CALM THE CHAOS! OVERCOMING OCD FOR TEENAGERS

BE THE BOSS OF YOUR OBSESSIVE THOUGHTS, COMPULSIVE BEHAVIORS AND TROUBLING EMOTIONS

CROSS BORDER BOOKS

CONTENTS

INTRODUCTION

> "I am in charge of how I feel, and today I am choosing happiness."
>
> — THE COACH

Does every neat and well-organized person have obsessive-compulsive disorder (OCD)? The answer is no. But many teens today claim they have OCD because they love to keep things tidy and organized. Being clean and well organized isn't a strange behavior, but when you feel a strong and continuous need to be perfect, you might have OCD. For example, cleaning a surface that has just been cleaned several times and reorganizing and rearranging items that have already been rearranged or organized. Also, people with OCD aren't the way they are because they enjoy doing things properly. Instead, they act that way because their brain forces them to do things perfectly.

If you are reading this book, you believe you can win your battle against OCD. As a teenager, you are probably facing other challenges, like finding your purpose, dealing with pressures from school, and coping with societal expectations. So adding OCD to the list is like stuffing a heavy load inside an already heavy backpack. But the good news is that you can learn to free yourself of this burden. And because you believe you can win this battle, you will eventually win it.

OCD might be characterized by odd behaviors and feelings like the fear that getting close to people would give you a disease or cleaning a surface twenty times in an hour. However, you aren't weird for showing these symptoms. It is normal for people to go through both good and bad experiences. And illnesses, whether physical or mental, are part of our human experience.

So has anyone ever called you a weirdo because of your quirks? Well, I'm here to tell you that they lied to you. I mean, just look at David Beckham, Justin Timberlake, Katy Perry, and Howie Mandel. I'm sure you know these people, but did you know they all have OCD? Well, they do, but it didn't stop them from achieving their dreams and succeeding in life.

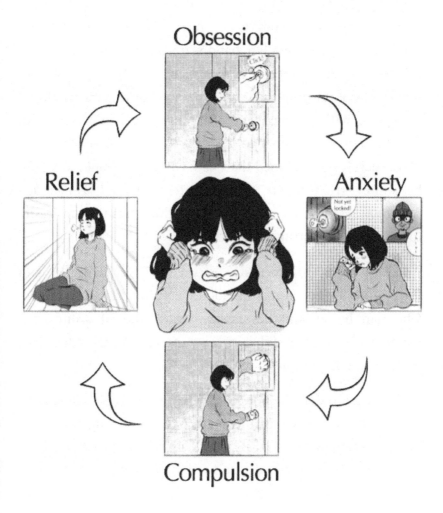

For example, David Beckham is among the most famous foot-ballers today, and he is almost as celebrated as football legends like Pele and Ronaldo. In 2006, Beckham shared his struggle with OCD in an interview. He explained that his OCD made him ensure that everything was always in its right position, even when they already were. And it became a constant obses-sion for him.

The next person on our list is Justin Timberlake. Although Timberlake was once a boy band star, today, he is a successful solo singer and actor. He's also a great comedian, and you would never imagine that someone as cool as him would be struggling with a mental disorder. But in his interview with *Collider*, Timberlake opened up about his mental health struggles. There, he mentioned that his OCD wasn't the kind where he simply tried to fix things. Instead, his OCD included Attention Deficit Disorder (ADD), which made him easily forget things and struggle to focus.

And how about pop megastar Katy Perry? Her struggles with OCD started right from childhood. Perry was raised in a strict Christian home, and her family always moved around the country. Sadly, she didn't receive much formal education, which led to her reading problems.

As Perry got older, she noticed she had some OCD tendencies, like buttoning her clothes to the top, color-coding them, and hanging them in a particular order. Perry also shared that, back then, her coping method was to find something, such as an object or a positive thought to focus on, especially when things went out of control.

One celebrity whose OCD experiences might inspire you is Howie Mandel. Howie is a showman, comedian, and currently one of the judges of *America's Got Talent*. He is also famous for his extreme fear of germs (germophobia), which inspired his book *Here's the Deal: Don't Touch Me*.

Mandel struggled a lot as a child because no one knew what to call his condition, as there was no diagnosis back then. So people named it after him instead—they simply called it "Howie." Although Mandel takes medication and undergoes therapy for his condition, he believes his situation is unique to him alone.

Fiona Apple, a writer and singer, is another celebrity who is outspoken about her OCD struggles. Apple's experiences show how much OCD can affect our lives. She struggled with OCD so much that she once didn't release a new album until after seven years because she didn't believe that her songs were perfect enough. Also, she doesn't travel much due to her disorder. In fact, she once shared that she doesn't go anywhere except Largo.

Even Leonardo DiCaprio, who acted as Howard Hughes in the biographical movie *The Aviator*, has his own OCD battles. Although the symptoms his character (Hughes) showed in the movie are more severe, Leonardo admits that he has been battling different compulsions. Some include walking through doors several times and the urge to step on chewing gum stains.

After reading the story of these celebrities, do you still feel like a weirdo? If you still do, I can understand. But, while I can't force you to stop feeling that way, I can promise you one thing —the journey this book will take you through will help you overcome your OCD.

As I said earlier, most teenagers don't know what OCD is all about. They often diagnose themselves with OCD simply because they like to see things neat, well placed, or organized. But OCD goes beyond all that, and I know firsthand the pain and frustration OCD causes for people who suffer from it.

OCD can be a confusing experience, as the victim finds themself fussing over every detail. In their mind, nothing is perfect until it is, and it rarely ever is. But in those rare moments when something feels perfect, they worry it might fall apart in the next few seconds.

When I struggled with germophobia, I avoided handling money and touching strangers. Then, when I got a brand-new water bottle, I would wash my hands and the bottle several times and still not be satisfied. I felt everything carried germs. And even though washing my hands made them clean, I feared they would become filthy once exposed to the environment again. It always made me anxious and unsatisfied. It also affected my peace and productivity, which led to other problems, like depression and anxiety.

I'm sure if I asked you to write about your OCD symptoms, they wouldn't be so different from mine. So I need you to know I understand what you are going through. But once you complete the journey this book is inviting you to, you will learn how to manage your OCD, just like I did.

We will walk this journey together. After all, my goal is to help you reach *your* goal, which is to break free from OCD. So for our journey to be successful, I'll add some worksheets for you at the end of each chapter. These activities will help you be intentional about your healing and self-improvement. What's more, they will help you get the best results in your healing journey. And like the celebrities I mentioned, you will also learn how to live and succeed despite your OCD.

When struggling with OCD, it's always nice to have someone who can relate to your experience. Someone who is also willing to go all the way with you. Someone like me.

In this book, I will share some helpful advice from my experience and research on teens of different ages and cultures. So I can promise you that every piece of information related to your experiences will be touched on in this book.

You chose to start this journey because you know your pain. Well, I want you to know I know your pain, too. And you aren't odd; only the OCD is. Also, every experience you have had isn't your fault, and you're not to blame for your OCD. You didn't do anything wrong to trigger it. You simply lived like everyone who is special in their own way. Today, many people with OCD have succeeded in life because they chose to pursue their dreams despite their OCD. So you have a long, beautiful path ahead of you, and I'll be with you every step of the way.

Now, let's get started!

1

A STUDY OF OCD

"*You are not your illness. You have an individual story to tell. You have a name, a history, a personality. Staying yourself is part of the battle.*"

— JULIAN SEIFTER

L et's start with some statistical facts about obsessive-compulsive disorder (OCD). Usually, scientists study mental health issues because people struggling with them are important, and they want to help them recover quickly. According to the American Academy of Child and Adolescent Psychiatry (AACAP), OCD usually starts in adolescence or early adulthood.

In fact, the AACAP found that at least 1 out of every 200 children and teens struggle with OCD. So basically, if there are 100 million children in a place, at least 500,000 would have OCD. Shocking, isn't it?

But what is OCD anyway? And what do we know about it?

AN OVERVIEW OF OCD

Obsessive-compulsive disorder (OCD) is a mental illness that affects the mind for a long time. This is why it is described as chronic or acute. Sadly, people who suffer from OCD usually experience uncontrollable obsessions and behaviors (also known as compulsions), which they feel forced to repeat all the time.

If you have OCD, you will usually notice one or two main symptoms: obsession and compulsions. And these two symptoms can affect your life negatively. For instance, they can interfere with your work, school, and relationship with your friends and family.

Obsessions are the thoughts you repeat in your head over and over again, the strong urges you feel, and the mental images that make you anxious. And you can experience obsession in any of the following ways:

- You are terrified of germs or contamination.
- You have some forbidden ideas or taboo thoughts relating to religion, sex, or harm.
- You have harmful thoughts about yourself or others.
- You love to see things properly arranged or in perfect order.

On the other hand, **compulsions** are behaviors that you repeat when you have OCD. Usually, you repeat these behaviors because of the obsessive thoughts you already have.

Now that we've explained what compulsions are, here are some examples of compulsions you may have:

- You might find yourself washing your hands too hard and too often
- You may often find yourself arranging things in a specific order or pattern
- You constantly check to see if things are in the right place, state, or condition. For instance, you might constantly check to see if the table is positioned correctly, if the switch is turned off, if the door is locked, or if the cooker is turned off
- You may repeatedly clean household objects
- You may also repeatedly count numbers

Everyone double-checks things occasionally, so being fussy does not automatically translate to having OCD. However, below are specific related things about people with OCD:

- They can't control how they think or behave, even when their thoughts or behavior are considered excessive.
- They spend an hour or more every day thinking about their obsessive thoughts or behaviors.

- They don't get any pleasure from acting on their urges or rituals but can feel momentary relief from their earlier anxiety.
- They experience major challenges in their daily lives because of these thoughts and behaviors.

Some people who experience OCD also deal with a tic disorder. A tic is basically a repetitive movement that is usually sudden, brief, and difficult to control. A good example is the random blinking of your eyes or similar kinds of eye movement. Other examples are grimacing, shrugging, and jerking your head or shoulders. All of these are examples of facial tics, but there are also vocal tics, such as repetitively clearing your throat, sniffing, or grunting.

Sometimes, these symptoms come and go. Over time, they might reduce or even become worse. Some people with OCD often try to help themselves by doing things that end up worsening their obsessions. Some even rely on drugs or alcohol to calm themselves. Adults who do these often know what they are doing isn't right. Though as a teenager, you may not realize that your behavior isn't normal. But your parents and teachers can easily notice this from observing you.

When you feel you have OCD, you should always discuss your symptoms with your doctor because if OCD isn't treated in time, it will affect most, if not all, aspects of your life.

RISK FACTORS OF OCD

OCD is a common disorder that affects people of all ages, including adults, adolescents, and children worldwide. Most people get their diagnosis when they turn 19. Boys usually have an earlier onset than girls, although there are cases where men were diagnosed after the age of 35. Experts haven't yet figured out the causes of OCD, but they know the risk factors, and three of them are listed below.

Genetics

If you have a first-degree relative, like a parent or sibling, that has OCD, you risk developing OCD yourself. Your risk would become much higher if this first-degree relative started experiencing OCD when they were a kid. Scientists are still exploring whether there is a link between genetics and OCD through different research, which could improve how OCD is diagnosed and treated.

The Brain's Structure and Functioning

In human biology, certain parts of the brain are responsible for thinking, planning, performing actions, voluntary movements, speech, consciousness, and emotional control. These parts are called the frontal cortex and subcortical structures, and research has shown that these two brain structures are different in OCD patients than in people without OCD. So, there might be a connection between OCD symptoms and the irregularities in these parts of the brain. But if there's a connection, sadly, it isn't clear yet. Then again, scientists are still researching, and once they figure out the causes of OCD, they can provide better treatment for it.

Environment

Some research suggests there's a connection between childhood trauma and OCD symptoms. Researchers are still trying to understand the extent of this connection. Still, the fact remains that the place you grew up and your experiences there can lead to OCD.

Also, scientists say that there are cases where children may develop OCD or signs of OCD after what they call "a streptococcal infection." You're probably wondering what a streptococcal infection is. Well, allow me to explain.

A streptococcal infection is an infection caused by a group of bacteria known as streptococcus (or strep, for short). These bacteria are of 20 different varieties and are divided into two main groups:

- Group A or strep A can be found on your skin's surface and inside your throat. They mostly cause infection in children and adults.
- The second group, group B or strep B, lives inside the digestive system and the female reproductive organ (the vagina). This group tends only to affect newborn children and cause more severe infections.

The type of OCD that develops because of streptococcal infection is called pediatric autoimmune neuropsychiatric disorders associated with streptococcal infections (PANDAS).

WHY IS OCD BECOMING RAPIDLY PREVALENT IN TEENS?

As a teenager dealing with OCD, you might struggle with stigma from your classmates or neighbors, and the thought of people calling you a "crazy person" or a "psycho" might make you reluctant to get a diagnosis. Another reason you might not want to get treated is that you're worried about the side effects of OCD medications. While all of these fears are valid, if you don't address them early, they can easily hurt your health and chances of getting treated.

Sometimes, some teens may know they have OCD, but because of how severe their OCD symptoms are, they feel it's pointless to seek treatment since they probably can't be treated anyway. If you are one of those teens who have given up on treatment, I recommend seeing a good therapist.

A good therapist will motivate you to take the right actions and reduce your negative feelings about getting treated. They will usually do this by helping you understand OCD better, and fortunately, this book will also guide you on your healing journey. However, your therapist gets to meet you personally and will be better able to give you the individual help you may need.

Earlier, I mentioned that most people get diagnosed with OCD when they turn 19. You may have noticed that even though OCD affects all ages, it's most common in teenagers. But do you know why?

There are many possible explanations for why OCD is prevalent in teenagers, but here are the most popular ones:

1. Teens have new things to obsess over

Teenagers suffering from OCD often struggle to accept the uncertainty of their thoughts. Your early teenage years might be the first time you would have issues relating to your sexual orientation, romantic relationships, physical changes, social life, and moral values. These issues often come with their uncertainties and are easy bait for the OCD mind to grasp and obsess over all the time. Naturally, teens start to make educated guesses about these issues affecting them as they grow older.

But it isn't easy when you are a teen with OCD because the fear that your guesses may be wrong could paralyze and frustrate you.

2. Teens are becoming more sensitive about being labeled

It's hard to find a teenager who loves being labeled, especially when the label relates to mental illness. Although OCD is treatable, it's always OK to talk to your parents or guardians about your OCD and fears if you aren't ready to be treated. Cognitive behavioral therapy is often seen as the most effective treatment for OCD, and receiving this treatment can make a huge difference. I understand that you may not want to associate yourself with a mental health diagnosis. Still, you should be open to receiving all the kindness and support your loved ones give you. It helps a lot.

3. OCD in teens isn't just about washing and checking things

Although most compulsive behaviors, such as checking locks, washing hands, or showering, are easy to identify, they are not always obvious. For instance, teens with violent, sexual, religious, or moral obsessions often respond to these obsessions by avoiding them or practicing mental rituals, like neutralizing their thoughts and reassuring themselves. So, like most teens with OCD, you might be lost in thought most of the time.

These signs are often easily misunderstood as depression or attention deficit disorder symptoms. Some people might even think you have a defiant personality. It isn't unusual to see teens at this point demanding that their loved ones accept their compulsions. However, this can reinforce or worsen their symptoms. Your family needs to be part of your treatment. They need to be involved from the beginning because they can help you reduce your compulsive behaviors.

4. Academic difficulty is an early sign

You may struggle with your academics at the onset of your OCD. When this happens, you might find yourself repeatedly reading or writing, excessively checking for mistakes, and displaying compulsive sluggishness while doing schoolwork. Other symptoms include being stuck with trying to be exact in your work, constantly seeking assurance from teachers regarding your work, and struggling to focus on your tasks due to mental rituals.

5. Teens are smarter than their OCD

As a teen, your brain is still strong, but psychologists say that your minds are fashioned differently. And it is one of the most unique and terrifying phases of maturity. For instance, because of how smart and energetic your brain is, you may constantly crave stimulation from video games or similar activities. Indeed, you are smarter than you may realize, and you are also a quick learner. Most teens are quite open to abstract thinking and prone to quick bursts of insights, and these insights lend themselves to a mindful and cognitive behavioral treatment technique.

For example, one technique tool, mindfulness, involves learning to observe and process your thoughts and feelings. Observing your thoughts is good for you since it helps you identify your feelings and understand your emotions better. It also teaches you to be self-aware, which is good for dealing with OCD. Cognitive therapy, on the other hand, consists of challenging distorted thinking patterns that can lead you to develop compulsive behaviors. Finally, behavioral therapy involves developing unique strategies to confront your fears and resist compulsive responses. As a teenager, you can take leadership roles in your treatment. All you need are the right tools.

6. The pandemic is fueling a rise in OCD

The Centers for Disease Control and Prevention (CDC) recently did a study that shows that teenagers are more prone to self-harm, drug poisoning, and psychosocial concerns during 2020, 2021, and 2022 than they were in 2019. This suggests that mental illnesses in teenagers have increased due to the pandemic; sadly, OCD is one of these illnesses.

In addition to CDC's research, new studies show that OCD symptoms have become more severe for many people during the pandemic. In fact, many hospitals have recorded numerous diagnoses during the pandemic, and the numbers keep growing.

It's not so surprising that the COVID-19 pandemic became a major stressor for OCD patients. The pandemic made everyone worry about getting infected, and OCD patients had it much worse. For example, did you often feel anxious after touching the rails on your steps or your door knob? Perhaps you began to worry that it might have been contaminated. Now imagine you had always feared contamination before the COVID-19 pandemic, which has infected more than 327 million people and killed 5.5 million people worldwide. Of course, your anxiety levels will spike.

THE MOST COMMON TOOLS TO DEAL WITH OCD

We will discuss some of these tools in detail in subsequent chapters, but let's look at them briefly. One of the most common tools to deal with OCD is DBT, which stands for "dialectical behavior therapy."

DBT is a technique that helps you learn how to deal with difficult emotions. It is based on the work of the renowned psychologist Marsha Linehan, who has worked with people experiencing borderline personality disorder (BPD) and constant thoughts of suicide.

DBT skills training comprises four parts: mindfulness, distress tolerance, emotion regulation, and interpersonal effectiveness. Together, these four tools are aimed at helping people who

- have anger issues;
- struggle with expressing anger; or

- experience irritability, anxiety, impulsiveness, episodic depression, chaotic relationships, stress, and emptiness.

And in the long run, they will help you manage your thoughts, emotions, and behaviors more effectively.

The core of mindfulness is to help you focus your mind and attention. Distress tolerance enables you to accept your current situation and develop your crisis survival skills, which will help you avoid behaviors that might land you in trouble. Emotional regulation skills involve learning to identify and label all the emotions you're experiencing; it also involves changing your emotions, identifying the obstacles that might try to stop you, and reducing emotional reactivity. Finally, emotional effectiveness will teach you strategies to use when you want to ask for what you need. For example, how to say no and cope with interpersonal conflict.

Mindfulness

Mindfulness is one of the fundamental DBT skills that will help you cope with mental and emotional stressors. Mindfulness is all about processing the present intentionally. For example, you could think about what's happening right now instead of worrying about yesterday or the future. It helps you become more aware of the present so you can shape your future. So it's an effective way to keep yourself from worrying about your past or future.

Mindfulness will help you discover who you are, what you need, and how you can manage your emotions. Moreover, mindfulness DBT skills have two parts: the "what" and the "how" skills.

The "what" skills refer to whatever you do to cope with your OCD, and they include the following:

- Observing things around you without labeling them
- Describing the things or people you observe
- Being present in everything you do

The "how" skills refer to how you do those things to cope, and they include the following:

- Not being judgmental; challenging negative thoughts and self-talk
- Being one-mindfully—that is, focusing on one thing at a time
- Effectively focusing on doing the things that work well for you instead of the things you think are right

The aim of practicing mindfulness skills is to help you develop a wise mind. Such a mind is a balanced combination of your emotion and your reason. In addition, it is about knowing your thoughts, being aware that they exist, and directing them to the right thing or idea. As the saying goes, "where focus goes, energy flows."

Interpersonal Effectiveness

This is another set of DBT skills that aims to help you build and maintain healthy relationships with yourself and those around you. Practicing this skill will help you speak up for your needs, set boundaries, and respect yourself.

For instance, when you say no, you are practicing an interpersonal skill because saying no helps you to care for yourself. Also, it is a way of saying to others, "This is what I really want."

There are three main goals for interpersonal effectiveness:

- **Objective effectiveness:** this has to do with getting what you want
- **Connection effectiveness:** this refers to building and maintaining your relationships
- **Self-respect:** this has to do with building self-respect

Distress Tolerance

Distress tolerance helps you deal with painful experiences or situations. So, the goal here is to help you find healthy coping mechanisms to deal with emotional pains.

Distress tolerance skills can help you deal with severe pain. For example, when you practice grounding techniques such as taking a cold shower or doing intense physical activity, you are engaging in distress tolerance skills. As you practice distress tolerance, you will move toward a state where you can easily accept your situations, emotions, and thoughts that you cannot change.

DBT skills will help you intentionally notice and accept things the way they are without trying to change them. But this doesn't mean that you justify that situation. Instead, it means that you accept the situation the way it is so that you can move on and not halt your life brooding over it.

Emotional Regulation

This is the fourth DBT skill, and it teaches us how to take control of our emotions instead of allowing them to control us.

Emotional regulation involves:

- checking reality;
- accepting emotions; and
- learning opposite actions of the behaviors that are associated with some specific emotions.

What do I mean by opposite actions here? Opposite actions involve doing the opposite of what your emotion wants or urges you to do. An example is when sad and self-critical thoughts overtake you, and your mind asks you to sleep in a dark room. The opposite action would be to get out of the house, get some sunlight, and gaze at the sunset.

Finally, as you practice opposite actions, you will take power away from your emotions instead of letting them control your life fully. In addition, doing this is an effective way to be aware of your feelings, so you must be intentional about taking only actions that will lead you through a different and positive path.

ACTIVITY

In this first activity, we will practice dealing with irrational thoughts that have the power to influence our feelings.

So, provide your answers to the questions in the box below.

What are you worried about?
Comment: Sometimes, the things you are most afraid of may be the least likely thing to happen.
How likely is it that your worry will come true? Give examples of experiences from your past or other evidence to support your answer.
Comment: If you stop believing in those fears and fueling them, you will eventually overcome them.
If your worry does come true, what's the worst that could happen?
Comment: We all go through moments where it feels like our world is crashing and that our greatest fear would consume us. But, I promise, it won't—not while you're focused on the light at the end of the tunnel.

If your worry comes true, what's most likely going to happen?

Comment: *You have to be positive no matter the type of evidence in front of you. Create your reality and make it cool, exciting, and positive.*

What are the chances you'll be OK if your worries come true?

In one week? ....%

In one month? ....%

In one year? ....%

2

THE INS AND OUTS OF DBT

"Even if we don't have the power to choose where we come from, we can still choose where we go from there."

— STEPHEN CHBOSKY

As we rounded off the last chapter, I briefly introduced you to dialectical behavior therapy (DBT). This chapter will teach you more about DBT, its pros and cons, and how it works.

WHAT IS DBT?

While dialectical behavior therapy is used to treat many mental health disorders, it is sometimes used to treat OCD, and I will explain how. I will also show you the difference between DBT and other treatments.

DBT is a type of cognitive-behavioral therapy (CBT) that focuses on how your feelings affect your behavior. Marsha Linehan developed this treatment method in 1970 to help people with borderline personality disorder and post-traumatic stress disorder (PTSD). But over the years, DBT has been used to treat different mental health conditions. The main difference between DBT and other treatments is that DBT encourages patients to accept all their thoughts—both the good and the bad.

THE FOUR KEY ASPECTS OF DBT

DBT has four skills that are heavily influenced by teachings from Buddhism. These skills include distress tolerance, emotional regulation, interpersonal effectiveness, and mindfulness; their goal is to help patients manage their daily lives.

During DBT skills training group sessions, facilitators will put you in a group and teach you these four skills one by one. As you learn, you'll be asked to share how you are making good use of your skills and how effective they are for reducing distress. Keep in mind that your facilitator will always test your problem-solving skills to assess how you will use them to tackle future challenges.

HOW DOES DIALECTICAL BEHAVIOR THERAPY WORK?

Therapists who use DBT to treat teenagers have one goal, and that's to strike a balance between acknowledging your challenges, realizing who you are, and understanding the benefits of change. Whoever your therapist is, they should be able to help you learn new skills that will help you manage your emotions better.

DBT's structures vary with each therapist, so the one you'll use depends on your therapist. Regardless, here are four sections you will usually find in DBT:

- DBT pre-assessment
- Individual therapy
- Skills training in groups
- Telephone crisis coaching

You might be wondering what all these terms mean. Well, just hang on a bit! I'm just about to shed some light on them.

DBT Pre-Assessment

Some therapists may choose to assess you before starting your DBT session. They usually do this to know if DBT suits you, so they may ask you several questions and explain how DBT works. It is now left for you to decide whether or not to go ahead with DBT. However, if you choose to give it a try, your therapist will brief you about the program and encourage you to commit to it.

Individual DBT

Individual DBT is when you have weekly sessions with your therapist. Mind you, each weekly session usually lasts for about 40 minutes.

Now, what are some benefits of individual DBT sessions?

- It helps you reduce suicidal thoughts and self-harming so that you can feel safe.
- It helps you curb behaviors hindering your healing.
- It will help you achieve your health goals and become the best version of yourself. "But how?" you might ask. Well, individual DBT enables you to identify and get rid of anything toxic to you, like a compulsion or an unhealthy relationship.

Some therapists might ask you to keep a journal to help you track your emotions and actions. Keeping a journal can also help you spot your behavioral patterns—that is, behaviors that you repeat in certain situations. Your therapist will ask you to bring your journal to your sessions so you two can decide what you need to work on during each session.

DBT Skills Training in Groups

In this session, your therapist will place you in a group of other clients and teach you some skills. But this isn't the same as group therapy. In group therapy, you share your problems with others. But when it comes to DBT skills training in groups, you learn like you're in a classroom.

The whole point of learning DBT skills is to help you improve your life daily. We have looked at mindfulness, distress tolerance, interpersonal effectiveness, and emotion regulation—these are four skills your therapist will teach you. Now, let's do a little recap on them below.

- Mindfulness is the practice of being completely aware of and focused on the present instead of worrying about your past or future.
- Distress tolerance is your ability to understand your emotions and manage them even in difficult situations, especially those that stress you a lot. And as you understand and manage your emotions during these trying situations, you don't respond to them with harmful behaviors.
- Interpersonal effectiveness is about knowing how to demand what you need. It is also about your ability to set boundaries while respecting yourself and others.
- Emotional regulation is about understanding your emotions, being aware of them, and fully controlling how you feel.

Mindfulness

Mindfulness is the practice of being completely aware of and focused on the present instead of worrying about your past or future.

Emotional Regulation

Emotional regulation is about understanding your emotions, being aware of them, and fully controlling how you feel.

Interpersonal Effectiveness

Interpersonal effectiveness is about knowing how to demand what you need. It is also about your ability to set boundaries while respecting yourself and others

Distress Tolerance

Distress tolerance is your ability to understand your emotions and manage them even in difficult situations, especially those that stress you a lot. And as you know and manage your feelings during these trying situations, you don't respond to them with harmful behaviors.

THE PROS AND CONS OF DBT

DBT has its advantages and disadvantages, but let's start with its benefits.

✚ So what are the pros of DBT?

1. It is evidence-based

DBT is based on evidence and not hearsay. Qualified researchers studied their clients, and the results have been amazing. So the chances of DBT working for you are very high.

2. It increases your self-worth and self-esteem

DBT skills will allow you to examine yourself and learn a lot about your strengths, not just your weaknesses. As a result, you will also discover the hidden talents you never knew you had. You will also learn to respect and believe in yourself.

3. It will help you reduce your suicidal and self-harming behaviors

DBT skills will teach you four sets of behavioral techniques to improve your behavior. These techniques will help you manage your emotions, handle distress, and live more mindfully. In the long run, when toxic or suicidal thoughts cross your mind, you will deal with them better.

4. Improved tolerance and emotional regulation

I've said several times that DBT can help you become more tolerant and in charge of your emotions. When you learn to manage your feelings, you will endure and deal with hard situations better than you could imagine.

5. DBT reduces anxiety, depression, trauma, and stress

In its own unique way, each DBT skill will help you reduce your anxiety, depression, stress, and trauma. And as you process your emotions and learn to live in the present, you'll avoid all the negative emotions that come from worrying too much.

6. DBT teaches you to set reasonable goals to improve your life

DBT will also help you to set goals that will improve the quality of your life. Your goals are there to help you put your vision in motion. Without them, you may struggle to live a happier and more fulfilled life. But luckily, DBT skills will give you all the tools you need to set achievable goals for yourself.

7.

Finally, as you practice DBT regularly, your maladaptive behaviors and thoughts will reduce. Maladaptive thoughts and behaviors affect the quality of our lives and relationships. So when you get rid of them, the quality of your life and relationships will naturally improve.

— Now that we've covered DBT's advantages, let's look at some of its disadvantages.

1. It may not work for everyone

Since we are all unique, our paths to recovery might not always be the same. So while one method might work for most teenagers, it might not always work for you. For example, some teenagers are more receptive to spiritual therapies because they are very spiritual, so DBT may not work for them if they have little faith in scientific methods. So it's OK if you try DBT and it doesn't work for you. There are still many other techniques you can try, which we will discuss later in this book.

2. It needs a significant time commitment

Not everyone has the level of patience DBT requires. For instance, if you don't see any progress early, you might think you can't be cured and consider giving up. But that's hardly ever true. You *can* be cured, only that it might take some time. And since DBT usually takes so much time, you must be willing to see it through to the end. So you must be committed to attending every session and doing your homework.

3. Not everyone is receptive to DBT

Not everyone may be receptive to DBT. Therefore, it is understandable and absolutely normal for them to go through the program and not make many changes. What this then means is that they should work with their therapists to find a more suitable program or better still, tweak the current program to suit their needs.

4. It is difficult to know who it will work for

Scientists who have tried to research DBT usually use small samples in their analysis, making it difficult to truly know who DBT can and can't work for. It is also hard to predict how long the effects will last. So while DBT may benefit you in several ways, the sad reality is that it may not work for you in the end.

THE HISTORY OF DBT

Originally, DBT was founded in the late 1970s by a suicide researcher named Marsha Linehan. Linehan actually didn't know about borderline personality disorder. But eventually, she came to learn about it. As a result, DBT is mostly known as a treatment for borderline personality disorder.

In the 1970s, Linehan started working with people who were suicidal. She explains that it was easy for her to receive a grant because she was the only scientist doing "randomized control trials" with people who had suicidal thoughts.

And so, her team of researchers often called hospitals in the area to send patients with the most severe suicidal and self-injuring behaviors. And they did. So, when these patients arrived, she would try to cure them using behavioral therapy. But, with time, Linehan found that behavioral therapy alone wasn't enough, especially since it didn't always work for the patients as she had hoped. For instance, some patients reacted negatively to the treatment by either getting angry or becoming more aggressive.

Back in the 70s and 80s, there were different approaches to treatments, such as behaviorism and humanistic approaches. So, she decided to try the humanistic approach that was most popular then, but that didn't work either. She kept on trying different treatments over and over again, but none of them worked.

Although Linehan hadn't found an effective treatment method, she still remained passionate about helping suicidal people. Maybe she was motivated by her struggles with mental illness. She once told the New York Times that she had suffered severe mental illness in her teens, so her desire and commitment to help her patients might have been personal.

When Linehan tried to use behaviorism to treat her patients, they would respond like the therapist accused them of being the problem. Behaviorism is said to be the model of change. So, each time Linehan gave her patients feedback on the different ways they could improve, they often felt like she was blaming them for their condition.

To understand what truly works, Linehan made her team of researchers observe the patients through a one-way mirror, take notes, and give her feedback. Eventually, they discovered that the patients often got upset when Linehan said or did certain things. Still, other things seemed to be fine. They did not necessarily find a second theory. Instead, they combined behaviorism and humanism to develop the concept now known as dialectical behavior therapy.

DBT originated with a nonjudgmental stance. So it made the patients and therapist equal rather than paint the patients as the problem or describe them as manipulative like people with borderline personality disorder are often said to be. Linehan's Zen training influenced her to create a balance between CBT and humanism. In fact, DBT was almost called Zen behavior therapy! While Linehan was still training, she found that many of the principles she was learning in Zen and meditation could be applied to her patients. And mindfulness was one of them.

So, to sum it up, dialectical behavior therapy (DBT) was developed by Marsha Linehan in the late 1970s. When it was designed, cognitive behavioral therapy (CBT) was still the most preferred treatment for most mental illnesses. But Linehan realized that her patients weren't gaining from CBT because it focused mostly on change and was too direct. Also, they felt they were being judged during CBT, and the program was too confronting and invalidating. So Linehan made a wise decision by adapting traditional CBT to make it more validating. And since then, DBT has effectively treated different mental health challenges, especially mood and anxiety disorders.

SO HOW DOES DBT HELP WITH OCD?

DBT helps teens struggling with OCD by teaching them to accept their feelings instead of judging them. As I said earlier, DBT can help you deal with the stressors of everyday life. It can also help you be more self-aware, improve your life, and lower your feelings of hopelessness—all of which are necessary to manage your OCD.

But your relationship with your therapist is just as crucial to your recovery. So you must learn to be honest about your thoughts, feelings, and behaviors; your therapist must create an environment free of shame or failure. We will learn more about your relationship with your therapist later in this book. This will help you feel safe and give you the confidence to trust your therapist with your deepest feelings. It will also encourage you to make long-lasting changes.

With DBT, you can trust that your feelings will be validated whenever you attend sessions and share your progress on how you've applied the therapy's principles so far.

In summary, DBT helps you overcome your OCD by

- helping you focus on acceptance;
- teaching you not to judge your feelings and that of others;
- helping you deal with stressors;
- improving the quality of your life;
- equipping you with DBT skills and self-control; and
- reducing intense emotions.

ACTIVITY

1. Describe your experience with OCD today.

✎...

✎...

✎...

2. While reading this chapter, what aspect of DBT caught your attention the most?

✎...

✎...

✎...

3. Do you feel DBT will work for you? Why?

✎...

✎...

✎...

✎...

TOOL #1—FIGHTING OCD WITH MINDFULNESS

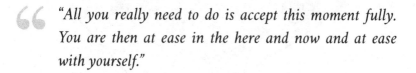

"All you really need to do is accept this moment fully. You are then at ease in the here and now and at ease with yourself."

— ECKHART TOLLE

What comes to your mind when you think of a hospital? I'll give you three guesses—pain, sickness, and anxiety. However, when we think of mindfulness and meditation, what usually comes to mind is peace, quiet, and healing. This shows that mindfulness and meditation have a place in our health and well-being.

Many health professionals and a lot of other documented scientific studies say that mindfulness has a strong healing effect. In fact, they say it can help you find inner peace even under pressure. And in today's world that's filled with so much stress and anxiety, finding someone who can stay calm under so much pressure is almost impossible. Therefore, the ability to stay calm under pressure could almost be considered a survival skill.

For instance, let's say your teacher suddenly asks you to recite a poem to the entire school. Would you feel calm or nervous? I'm willing to bet that you would be scared. And what if all your friends got fancy toys and clothes for Christmas, while you got some hand-me-downs from your older relatives. Would you be happy for your friends or a little jealous? In one of her TEDx talks, Axialent's advisory board member Dr. Shauna Shapiro said something funny but true. She said if you can love everyone unconditionally and always be content, then you're probably a dog. Sometimes, we are overwhelmed by emotions we cannot control. For example, emotions of fear, jealousy, or anger. And this is because our minds have wandered to places they shouldn't be in. The Dog in Shapiro's analogy may just be the most mindful creature around, that is why it can love its owner unconditionally. It's a joke, but still, this chapter's lessons on mindfulness will open your mind to a new way of dealing with situations that would've otherwise occupied you with negative emotions.

The truth is, many of us have unrealistic standards of perfection that we hold ourselves to. And we often punish ourselves when we don't meet those standards. But you aren't meant to be perfect, you know? If you were, you wouldn't need anyone in your life to support you. The truth is that achieving perfection is impossible, though achieving transformation is possible. We learn and grow daily, and everything we learn somehow transforms us. But then, transformation can be positive or negative depending on your choices, actions, and the things and people you allow into your life. Even so, you have the power to change, learn, grow, and improve your mind and character. And this growth doesn't depend on your situation.

In my experience studying human behavior, I've learned that teenagers can intentionally change for the good. And practicing mindfulness is one of the most effective ways to do this. Mindfulness is important, but practicing it may not be as easy as you think. It's not easy to stay present.

For instance, how often did you notice your mind wandering off while reading this chapter? You're not alone. Even while writing this book, my mind drifted off a few times. We all get distracted now and then, and some more often than others. In a recent study, Harvard University researchers found that the human mind wanders on average 47% of the time. Just look at that! Nearly half your entire life is lost in a different world outside reality. In other words, you spend nearly half your life absent from reality. So what is mindfulness, and how can it help?

AN OVERVIEW OF MINDFULNESS

Mindfulness is all about teaching your mind to be present in your current situation without judging yourself. When practicing mindfulness, always ensure that you aren't clinging to another moment in time. Earlier, when we talked about DBT, we learned that mindfulness involves observing, describing, and engaging yourself in the present and without self-criticism.

It is about doing one thing at a time, especially something that works for you and gives you just what you need at that moment. Again, it is about being in the present. And what do I mean by being in the present? Now, take a deep breath and think of something, perhaps a favorite time in the past, for three minutes and observe your thoughts. Notice how hard it is to remain with that particular thought. Now imagine that thought were a pet puppy. You make it sit, but suddenly it wanders off, so you lovingly bring it back again, multiple times. Our thoughts are like that. So, part of the practice of mindfulness is to help us stay in the present and keep our thoughts from wandering.

Mindfulness will help you become aware of your thoughts, feelings, and distractions. Sometimes, when practicing mindfulness, you'll need to focus on something specific. Other times, you might need to narrow your attention. Finally, there are times when you will need to notice everything surrounding you or simply broaden your attention.

To get the best from DBT, you need to practice the necessary skills. And mindfulness is no exception. Mindfulness is key in helping you heal faster when you are ill. In the long run, it can help you improve and build a life worth living.

WHY DOES MINDFULNESS MATTER IN GENERAL?

One thing you might notice about OCD is that it sometimes overwhelms you with your emotions. These emotions could be the anxiety that comes from constantly trying to be perfect, or the anger that consumes you when someone leaves a smear on a place you have cleaned a million times. It could also be the fear that overwhelms you when you feel you haven't locked the door even after checking for the umpteenth time. If this is the case with you, mindfulness is your surest bet to help you deal with these uncomfortable feelings.

If you could just take a step back and observe what's happening around you, then you would be less likely to be caught unawares by emotions you can't control.

Mindfulness also helps teenagers struggling with addiction and compulsion break unhealthy behavior patterns. Now, if you want to be mindful, start by paying attention to what is happening *inside* you. For instance, you could observe the following:

- Your thoughts
- Your feelings
- Your sensations
- Your impulses

You could also pay attention to what is happening *outside* of you. For instance, you could observe what you can see, hear, smell, or touch.

IMPORTANCE OF MINDFULNESS TO TEENS WITH OCD

Mindfulness gives teenagers the power to manage their focus and emotions. And as you manage these things better, you will learn not to act or react based on fear, impulse, habit, or unstable emotions.

But these aren't the only reasons mindfulness is so important.

If you practice mindfulness regularly, you'll

- reduce distraction and absent-mindedness;
- improve your emotional regulation skills;
- increase the activities in the part of your brain that are associated with positive feelings;
- reduce your anger and irritability;
- lower your depression and anxiety; and
- improve your immune function.

THE LINK BETWEEN MINDFULNESS AND DBT

Now, let's dive into the relationship between mindfulness and DBT. I have said time and again that mindfulness involves bringing your mind to the present. So imagine that your mind is lost in thought; how do you redirect your thoughts back to the present. With mindfulness, of course!

DBT mindfulness is a new feature of mindfulness practice, and it is called mindfulness without judgment. When you practice nonjudgmental mindfulness that involves self-awareness, you'll be better suited to address your thoughts, feelings, and behaviors. What's more, you will do this without invalidating yourself. Unfortunately, self-invalidation is responsible for the emotional dysregulation that many teenagers experience too often.

As I said at the beginning of this chapter, practicing mindfulness isn't always easy. In fact, very few teenagers dedicate a small fraction of their day to being mindfully engaged in the present. Usually, many teenagers disconnect from their everyday experiences by thoughts that remind them how hard those experiences are. Or thoughts we use to escape reality and transport our minds to several fantasies.

My teenage years were the absolute worst; they were the times when I was most distracted. As teens, we are conditioned to engage more with our thoughts than our reality. As a result, we neglect our problems. And if we aren't mindful of our problems, how can we know how to solve them?

HOW DOES MINDFULNESS FIT INTO DBT AND CBT?

Dialectical behavior therapy targets emotional dysregulation. In teenagers, emotional dysregulation is caused by little or insignificant things and people's judgment of the events. Confused? Well, let me explain better.

Let's say your friend Mark has a job that he is somewhat happy doing. Now, imagine that the job involves selling shoes in a store. Mark loves shoes, so he feels like he's in the right place. However, he hates arranging the shoes on the right display shelves. He finds it boring and exhausting. Now, let's say he has to rearrange or sort out the shoes for 30 minutes of a seven-hour shift. Then, as he begins to sort out and arrange these shoes, his mind begins to form negative opinions about arranging shoes, like *This is tiring. This is a waste of my time. What a terrible job.*

So instead of focusing on arranging the shoes, Mark's mind is sparking negative emotions about this part of his job, which will create other negative emotions, like resentment, anger, or hopelessness. And the worst part is that these negative emotions could affect the rest of his day. So what should have been a delightful and productive day eventually becomes a stressful and annoying day.

Instead of tolerating 30 minutes of a boring chore, Mark would spend the rest of the day in a foul mood, resenting every aspect of his job and feeling anxious at some point. Being in a bad mood for most of the day and the days that follow is no fun, so Mark may start feeling miserable. Eventually, he may say, "I can't take this anymore," and quit his job. So you see, something as basic as arranging shoes developed into something causing him so much stress.

So what is the best way to deal with this issue? Well, the best solution would be to approach the stressful task positively. For example, accepting the situation and being willing to do the job without being judgmental. So if you were in Mark's shoes (pun definitely intended), once you notice negative emotions build-ing, switch your mind back to rearranging the shoes. Allow yourself to enjoy the leathery feel and fresh smell of new shoes. Admire the quality and beauty of the shoes and focus on the styles and design of each shoe. As you do this, try to describe the feeling you're getting. Name them using different descrip-tive words.

When you allow yourself to fully engage in a task and repeat-edly switch your mind to it, you will make it harder for negative emotions to overwhelm you. As a result, what was once a hard, boring task would seem easier and more fun.

DIVING INTO MINDFULNESS

Like other aspects of DBT, mindfulness has its pros and cons. But let's first look at the pros.

✚ The Pros of Mindfulness

1. It enriches your life

Practicing mindfulness regularly will add more value to your work and life. For example, you will be able to concentrate more in school, participate better in group activities, and be more productive at home, school, and everywhere else.

2. It helps you enjoy your tasks

Like I explained in Mark's case, mindfulness will help you enjoy doing tasks that would have otherwise been hard and boring. Instead of being distracted by the challenges, we can focus on the good parts of the task. In the end, this will help us achieve the best results from our jobs.

3. It fosters better connection and communication

Mindfulness will help you connect more with the present and your feelings, which will allow you to complete your tasks faster and save yourself from the stress of negative feelings.

4. It improves your focus

Mindfulness will help you improve your level of focus. So, instead of fixing your mind on things or feelings that will distract you, mindfulness will help your mind prioritize what needs to be done over anything else at the moment.

5. It regulates your moods and emotions

Mindfulness is one way to regulate and improve your moods and emotions. "How?" you might ask. Well, it teaches you to focus on a happier present than an uncertain future and painful past.

6. It helps you cope with stress

Mindfulness is great for coping with stress. Usually, stress comes from anxiety and worry. And we often feel these emotions due to our negative beliefs about what we are doing or what needs to be done. But after removing these negative beliefs, you will manage stressful situations better and have a more positive outlook on life.

7. It helps you solve problems better

When your mind wanders away, you will create room for problematic emotions. These emotions could distract you and make it hard for you to deal with challenges effectively. But with mindfulness, you can focus completely on each problem and solve them one at a time.

— The Cons of Mindfulness

1. It requires perseverance and dedication

Mindfulness takes conscious dedication before it can be effective. And so, if you aren't persistent enough, you might give up before you even start. It's not easy to be in the present consistently. You will have to try several times before it becomes part of you.

2. It can increase frustration

To practice mindfulness, you need to be nonjudgmental and fully present. Mindfulness also demands that you focus greatly on the present. But as you do this, you may notice everything and everyone in an unhealthy way. And since mindfulness encourages you to avoid negative emotions, you could end up suppressing anger and other emotions that seem nonjudgmental. These repressed feelings could then frustrate you more.

3. It doesn't take away your problems

Mindfulness is certainly not a cure-all, but it can help. Yes, it can help you deal with the negative emotions resulting from OCD and manage your OCD better. But for many people, it only provides a temporary fix.

The Main Skills of Mindfulness

Now, let's look at some of the main skills of mindfulness.

1. Observe

First, try to observe your external surroundings. Then, observe how your outside environment (the trees, the breeze around you, the furniture or light in your room) interacts with your internal surroundings—that is, your thoughts and feelings. How do they make you feel? Become aware of all these elements and focus on what is happening around you.

2. Describe

As you observe what is happening around you, try to name everything you can see. You can also name and describe the feelings these things evoke. For example, do they make you feel happy? Then describe the feeling as "joy." Do they make you feel uneasy? Then describe the feeling as "awkward."

3. Participate

At this point, you must be fully involved in what is happening because multitasking is not the great skill it's made out to be. Once we start practicing mindfulness, that's usually when it's most tempting to get distracted. So whatever you do as your own form of self-care, do it with your full attention. Whether you're watching a movie, washing your clothes, cleaning the bathroom or kitchen sink, or reading a book, do it all with your maximum attention.

4. Nonjudgmental stance

As humans, we naturally judge everything and everyone (including ourselves) as good or bad, so it might be hard to practice mindfulness without making judgments. But then mindfulness helps us focus on the facts by removing these judgments.

Taproot Therapy explains how best you can do this. According to them, If you notice a tightness or discomfort in your chest due to anxiety, a judgmental stance would be, "I feel awful. This is embarrassing. Everyone is looking at me, and it's just making me feel even worse." However, a nonjudgmental stance would be, "My chest is feeling tight, and it's making it hard to breathe."

5. One-mindfully

One-mindfully means focusing on one task at a time. We live in a busy world that may often require you to multitask, but this can be so hard to do sometimes. So if you are reading a book, do just that. And if you are watching a movie, then do just that. Don't scroll through social media while watching a movie or play a mobile game while watching a movie.

6. Effectiveness

The idea of effectiveness is to simply do what works for you. So if you notice something isn't exactly working for you and making you feel worse than before, stop doing it. Instead, do something else that's more rewarding and satisfying. Sometimes we have to give a treatment a chance by pushing through some initial resistance. We need to distinguish between things causing us a bit of pain and things that don't really work for us.

HOW DOES MINDFULNESS HELP OCD?

We've talked so much about mindfulness in this chapter, and you're probably wondering how it is helpful for OCD. Well, then, let's look at three ways mindfulness can help you deal with your OCD:

1. Mindfulness decreases anxiety

Mindfulness is an excellent way to reduce anxiety because it encourages you to focus on the moment without passing judgment. It also teaches you to process and accept your fears without attaching meaning to them or letting them overwhelm you.

2. It emphasizes acceptance of thoughts

Mindfulness also helps with OCD because it teaches you to embrace your thoughts. So whenever you notice an intrusive thought, allow it to exist in your mind, but don't give it any weight. Allow yourself to experience the thought without judging it. Don't change the thought or try to make it disappear. Instead, wait until it goes away on its own. For example, "Everyone's staring at me!" Instead of escalating "They're all talking about me and laughing at me" try "Oh, I recognise you, well I'm just going to ignore you and carry on so hang about or don't, it's up to you." You see? Easy!

3. Removes negative emotions and thoughts

Mindfulness will help you with your OCD because it's known to remove negative emotions and thoughts. Since mindfulness encourages you not to fixate on these thoughts, they will come and go on their own. Let's use the image of a leaf gliding down a river. As you stare at the river, you will notice the current carrying the leaf until it wanders off beyond your sight. Each thought is a leaf and you can observe it floating past. Just acknowledge it and let it go on.

This is much better than spending most of your time fighting the thought or going back and forth. You are simply ignoring the thought and giving it no room to breed.

THE MINDFULNESS WORKSHEET

Now, let's look at some activities to help you practice mindfulness better.

This worksheet will help you understand mindfulness much better. You will also understand the self-examination skills that come with practicing it, which will also help you practice it more consistently.

To begin this mindfulness meditation, shift your awareness to the following:

- Your head, chest, and belly and how each of them feels as you reflect on them

- The emotions that you can associate with your gut feelings
- When and where you can apply increased mindfulness in your day-to-day life

Mindfulness Exercises

Reflect on an event that hindered your hopes, dreams, or plans. What happened? Let your hand flow freely as you write down what's on your mind.

Now, read your description of the event you narrated above. Which descriptive words stand out to you, and why (for example, you may have used words like anger, painful, annoying, shy, dejected, etc. in your description)? Also, what's their energy like (positive or negative energy), and how do they make you feel?

Can you retell this story so that its energy is neutral (tell the story in a way that it does not make you feel excited or annoyed but just casual)? What sentences would you change? And what words would you add or remove?

When you narrate your experience of a difficult situation you once found yourself in, do you feel overwhelmed, victimized, or hopeless? Or do you become defensive, argue with your experience, or feel self-righteous? Again, none of this is to make you "right" or "wrong." It is simply a tool for self-exploration.

Teen Meditation Exercise to Boost Self-Confidence

This meditation exercise is for every teenager. So whether you're just thirteen or nineteen, this exercise will guide you to relax and learn to trust yourself:

First, sit on the ground with your legs crossed. Ensure that your spine is straight. You may sit on a chair if you're not comfortable on the ground—just ensure that you sit upright throughout the session. You may also lie down and relax or try different positions to see which is best for you during the meditation.

So, to begin, focus on your breath.

Breathing is our most important exercise because it keeps us alive. And most of us can't go longer than two minutes without breathing. Yet, you probably go through your day without noticing you are breathing.

Now, let's begin with a breath exercise by taking five full deep breaths - you can breathe in through the nose. While you do this, allow each breath to fill you with energy, and as you exhale, allow yourself to relax deeply.

Now, take five breaths, but do it with purpose. I'll show you how:

1. Inhale fully and expand your belly and chest at the same time. Hold your breath for a while, then exhale. As you do this, allow yourself to embrace the relaxing feelings washing over you.
2. Inhale again—fill your lungs with fresh oxygen. Now hold your breath for a few seconds, then exhale again. And as you do this, allow the wave of relaxation to sweep over you.

Do #1 and #2 three more times.

The Body Scan Exercise

What is a body scan exercise? Well, it involves noticing every part of your body while maintaining a particular posture. Here we go:

You can sit straight or lie down for this meditation. But whichever position you take, ensure that your spine is straight. Then, try to use your hands and your mind to connect to and feel around the parts of your body touching the ground. Feel free to open or close your eyes during this session. Simply observe the connection between your body and the ground. Then, allow your body to rest more downward.

Feel a sensation; imagine the earth reaching out to you and connecting its energy with yours.

Next, notice your toes. Even if you don't feel a sensation, look for a small sign of awareness that your toes exist. For example, it could be a slight tingling. Next, be aware of your feet, then be mindful of your heels and ankles.

Now, notice your shins, calves, and front and back knees, then embrace every sensation that arises. Next, notice your thighs and your hamstrings. Then, shift your focus to your hips and explore the sensation in your pelvis, glutes, front, and behind. After that, be aware of how your belly moves in rhythm with your breath.

Finally, be aware of the shoulders. Then, ease your shoulders and explore the right, left, front, and back sides of your body.

The Visualization Exercise

Visualization, also known as guided imagery, involves fixing yourself in a meditative state. In this exercise, you will also need to use all your senses and imagine a particular scene as vividly as possible. You can try different visualization techniques, but we will focus on one in this chapter.

I call this visualization technique "breathing in colors," and I'll show you how to use it to reduce stress and improve your mood.

You may decide to close your eyes or leave it open, depending on your preference. To begin, think of something you'd like to draw to your life. It could be a positive feeling or energy. Next, assign a color to this emotion or energy, but make sure you choose a color you like or find interesting. Then with each breath you take, simply visualize this feeling or energy washing over you.

In the following chapter, I will teach you how to deal with your OCD with the next tool on the list—distress tolerance.

FROM ALL OF US AT CROSS BORDER:

So far, how has this book been helping you?

Please leave your comments as a review on Amazon.

You will help us spread the word about OCD and create new resources to support mental health.

Just go to the page for this book on Amazon and scroll down to Customer Reviews. On the left side you will see Customer Reviews and under that the button **"Write a Customer Review."**

We truly appreciate your contribution.

4

TOOL #2—DISTRESS TOLERANCE

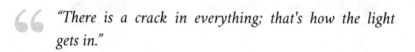 *"There is a crack in everything; that's how the light gets in."*

— LEONARD COHEN

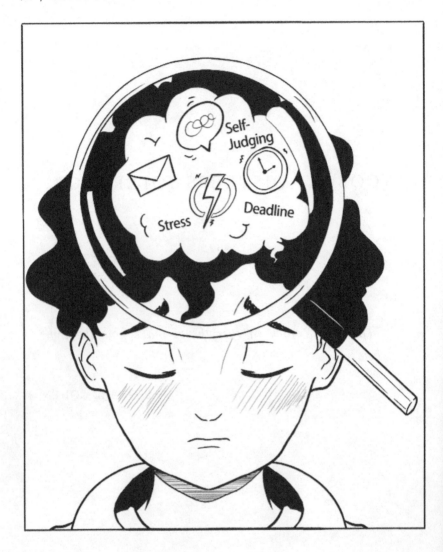

WHAT IS DISTRESS TOLERANCE?

Distress tolerance is a skill and intervention in dialectical behavioral therapy (DBT). In this intervention, teens learn to manage their distress in healthy ways. Practicing these skills will help you handle situations you have little or no control over and also teach you how to work on your response.

In other words, distress tolerance is your ability to manage those emotions that cause you distress. It is also your ability to survive an emotional situation without making things worse. If you have low distress tolerance, you will easily become over-powered by stressful situations. Not only that, but you may also turn to unhealthy behaviors to cope with challenging or annoying situations.

WHY IS DISTRESS TOLERANCE USED IN DBT?

Distress tolerance is used in DBT because it helps people likely to become overwhelmed with negative emotions. If you have a low distress tolerance, even the smallest amount of stress could overwhelm you. Plus, you could end up reacting to the stress with negative behaviors.

Usually, the common way to deal with this is to stay away from painful situations. However, in the distress tolerance of DBT, teens being treated learn that, sometimes, pain cannot be avoided. So the best solution is to learn to tolerate your distress.

Now, here is another fun fact: distress tolerance has a key ingredient called radical acceptance. Basically, radical acceptance is when you experience and accept a situation or reality you can't change. While doing this, make an effort to be less vulnerable to difficult or long-lasting negative emotions. And the best way to achieve this is to totally avoid being judgmental. Also, do not fight reality.

WHY DOES DISTRESS TOLERANCE MATTER FOR TEENS WITH OCD?

Distress tolerance matters for teens with OCD in several ways, but what are these ways? For one, teens with OCD often prefer to stick to a strict schedule. Also, they usually have obsessive interests and are easily overpowered by what psychologists call "sensory overloading situations." Let me briefly explain what this term means. A sensory overload is caused by a sensory processing disorder (SPD), and people with autism and OCD may experience this. Unfortunately, teens with SPDs don't normally respond to environmental stimulation because they are over-responsive or under-responsive. For example, you might be overstimulated by noise around you that could make you react in extreme ways such as screaming in anger or pain. So, in other words, sensory overload is when something around you overstimulates one or more of your senses. For example, it could be a very loud TV, noise and smell from a cafeteria, or a crowded room. Therefore, you seem to be receiving information from your environment into your senses. And this information is too much for your brain to process, which triggers extreme reactions from you.

It is called sensory hypersensitivity when teens are too responsive (or over-responsive). But when they are under-responsive, it is called sensory hyposensitivity.

These challenges teens with OCD face in regulating their emotions can trigger several behavioral problems, like tantrums, aggression, and self-harm. Many options to help teens cope with stress and emotional regulation require them to avoid painful experiences that could trigger these difficult emotions. But distress tolerance is different because it encourages you to accept that some level of discomfort is necessary and can be dealt with healthily.

What's more, distress tolerance can help you regulate the feelings you are nurturing inside. It can also help you manage your stress and reduce behaviors that can hurt you and those around you.

THE INS AND OUTS OF DISTRESS TOLERANCE

Before making decisions, we usually weigh their pros and cons. This skill can help you make better decisions, especially when faced with two hard options, and it is used in distress tolerance. The objective when using this skill is for you to understand that it is OK to accept your reality and endure your distress. Usually, when you do this, you will experience better results. But when you reject your reality and refuse to tolerate distress, the result is usually negative emotions.

So let's begin by looking at some of the pros and cons of distress tolerance.

Pros and Cons Activity

First, try to assess the problem before you. For instance, if the problem involves a harmful or negative behavior you're trying to avoid, observe the behavior for a while. Then, ask yourself questions like: "How can this behavior benefit me in the short and long term?" "Is this behavior inconsistent with my goals, or is it damaging?"

Next, list the behavior's pros and cons and compare each advantage to the opposite disadvantage. Better yet, list them in your journal or somewhere you see a lot, as this will help you practice the skill repeatedly and be more prepared for anything.

As you'll soon find out, the pros and cons of distress tolerance are slightly different from the normal pros and cons. In the normal pros and cons, you simply evaluate the advantages and disadvantages of doing or not doing something. Similarly, in distress tolerance, you assess the pros and cons of doing *and* not doing something. The goal is to help you see that every emotion you feel can negatively and positively impact you.

Below are some "pros and cons" activities about whether or not to do something or feel somehow. I've done the first two for you, so try to do the rest yourself.

1. Coping

	Pros	Cons
Coping	• I'll feel better eventually. • I'll challenge myself to get through a difficult situation. • I might succeed in changing my state of mind and improving without using too much energy.	• I'll need to put in a lot of effort, which might end up discouraging me from trying again and worsening my mood. • I may not get the attention people would give me if I weren't coping well.
Not coping	• I don't get to experience the disappointment of trying and failing. • I'll feel more comfortable because I'm used to distress. • The temporary satisfaction of punishing myself is more	• If I don't try to cope, I might not get the chance to overcome this negative emotion.

2. Feeling successful

	Pros	Cons
Feeling successful		
Not feeling successful		

3. Feeling relaxed

	Pros	Cons
Feeling relaxed		
Not feeling relaxed		

4. Escaping negativity

	Pros	Cons
Escaping negativity		
Not escaping negativity		

5. Avoiding a crisis

	Pros	Cons
Avoiding a crisis		
Not avoiding a crisis		

6. Feeling judgmental

	Pros	Cons
Judging my situation		
Not judging my situation		

7. Self-harm

	Pros	Cons
Harming myself		
Not harming myself		

8. Irritability

	Pros	Cons
Feeling irritable		
Not feeling irritable		

THE SKILLS OF DISTRESS TOLERANCE

Here, we will look at other distress tolerance skills.

1. TIPP

TIPP stands for Temperature, Intense Exercise, Paced Breathing, and Paired Muscle Relaxation. This distress tolerance skill will draw you closer to a wiser and more stable mind so that you can have more constructive thoughts, make better choices, and cope with OCD better. Now, let's explore each of its elements below:

- **Temperature:** When you become upset, your body usually feels hot. While this is perfectly normal, you can counter it by splashing cold water over your face, holding an ice cube, or allowing the air conditioner in your home to blow on your face. Sometimes, the best way to cool down emotionally is to cool down physically.
- **Intense Exercise:** If you want to match your intense emotions, do intense exercises. You do not have to be a sprinter or the fastest runner in your school. You could simply run from one end of your street to another or jump into a pool and swim for a few minutes. Another option is to do jumping jacks till your muscles are all fired up. As you do all this, your oxygen flow will increase, and your stress levels will reduce.
- **Paced Breathing:** This exercise might sound strange to many teenagers dealing with OCD, but it does work effectively. Controlling your breath can have a strong

impact on reducing your anxiety. Breathing exercises are very helpful, and there are different types that you can try. So if you find one you like, try to practice it regularly. Nevertheless, I suggest you try this breathing method called "box breathing." In this method, each breathing interval is four seconds long. So you take in air for four seconds, hold it in for four seconds, and release it for another four seconds. In the end, breathing steadily will help you reduce your body's flight or fight response.

- **Paired Muscle Relaxation:** This method requires you to tighten a voluntary muscle, relax it, then let it rest for a while. After doing this, you will notice the muscle will become more relaxed than before you tightened it. This is because relaxed muscles don't need much oxygen; therefore, your heart rate and breathing will slow down. When you try this technique, focus on a group of muscles, like the muscles in your arms. Make sure you tighten your muscles for five seconds. After that, release the tension and let the muscle relax. As you do this, you will feel more comfortable and relaxed.

2. Acceptance

Acceptance activities are designed to help you manage your emotions until you can resolve the problem. Now, let's look at each of them:

IMPROVE

You can use the DBT skill, IMPROVE, to endure your emotion until the pain subsides. Improve stands for Imagery, Meaning, Prayer, Relaxation, One thing in the moment, Vacation, and Encouragement. This distress tolerance technique can be used anywhere and anytime you need to tolerate a situation that is hard to change. You should practice this skill in regular situations. When you do this, you'll see how they become natural for you when you face bigger challenges.

- **Imagery:** Imagine that you have just successfully dealt with a hard challenge. And now that the problem is over, you see yourself as a wiser and more accomplished teenager. By doing this, you are definitely trying to help yourself change the situation's outcome in your favor.
- **Meaning:** You can also find meaning in difficult situations. To do this, think about some of the lessons you can take from this situation. For instance, maybe the situation will make you more empathic. Or it might even help you build better relationships and usher you on a new path toward healing.
- **Prayer:** You can pray in any way that works for you. For instance, you could pray to a higher power, like God, or you could pray to the universe. The main idea is to surrender your problems and ask for help to tolerate your challenges for much longer.
- **Relaxation:** Usually, our fight-or-flight instincts make us tense up before stressful situations. To deal with this,

you should engage in activities that will help you to relax and calm you down psychologically. These activities include deep breathing, yoga, warm baths, or strolling in a park.

- **One thing in the moment:** It is important to stay in the moment, and you can do this by letting go of anxiety about your past and future. Including old or future problems in your current situation will only increase your stress and heighten your emotions.
- **Vacation:** Vacations can help you take a break from all the disturbance and stress around you. You can go with your parents or an older sibling or join a school trip. This works as well. But while you're out vacationing, be in the moment. Don't let your mind linger beyond the events happening on your vacation.
- **Encouragement:** You don't always have to wait for someone outside to encourage you. You can also encourage yourself from within. "But how can I do this?" you might ask. Well, you can start by repeating positive phrases like: "I can do this" or "I got this." In the end, you will be surprised by how much you can encourage yourself.

Self-Soothing

This might be the easiest activity to practice. If you want to increase your distress tolerance, especially in crises, try using your body's senses by practicing self-soothing. This can help you reduce the effect of your negative emotions on you. For instance, you can soothe yourself by using your sense of sight;

to do this, look around your room and observe each object's colors and texture. You can also self-soothe your hearing by listening to various sounds—like birds chirping, music, trees swaying in the wind, etc.

You can self-soothe through your sense of taste by eating ice cream or other tasty food, but make sure you are fully focused on that food. Also, you can self-soothe through touch by running your fingers through your hair. Finally, you can self-soothe through smell and movement.

Radical Acceptance

In radical acceptance, instead of fixating on things you can't change or control, you accept them as they are. What's more, you learn to let go of those things, including feelings of regret, bitterness, and anger.

THE DISTRESS TOLERANCE WORKSHEET

Now, I want to show you a list of crisis survival activities that will help you improve your distress tolerance.

Crisis survival skills—self-soothe with six senses:

- **Sight:** Visit your favorite places and take in all the views there. You can also pick a picture book, encyclopedia, or other books, then engross yourself in the pictures.
- **Hearing:** Play your favorite song and pay attention to its rhythm and lyrics. Listen to the rain when it falls,

and allow the sounds of nature to fill your mind and ears.

- **Taste:** Eat your favorite food or snack and drink nonalcoholic drinks. While you do this, be deeply buried in the experience. Think of the taste of the food and beverages in your imagination, then savor the experience.
- **Touch:** Take a warm bath, and try to feel the warmth with every part of your body. You could also pet your dog or teddy bear, or if you're feeling bold, you could give someone a tight hug.
- **Smell:** You could visit a park and bask in the fragrance of flowers. You could also get a new, nicely scented lotion or perfume.
- **Movement:** To self-soothe through movement, you can dance, rock yourself gently, or do yoga. Even something as simple as stretching your bones can go a long way.

Distress Tolerance Exercises

1. Paced breathing

As I said earlier, controlling your breathing is one way to relax your body. Now, let's try it out.

To practice this exercise, first, breathe through your nose for five seconds, then breathe out for ten seconds. Next, you can try box breathing, which I explained earlier. As you breathe, pause and hold your breath for four seconds. Try this over and over again. The final technique is the 4-4-8 breathing technique. You can do this by inhaling through your nose for four counts, holding your breath for another four counts, then exhaling for eight counts. In the end, try to exhale, purse your lips and listen as your breath releases.

2. Muscle relaxation

This is also called Paired Muscle Relaxation (PMR). Focus on a pair of muscles, like your toes on both feet, and notice as they become tense as you breathe in. You'll also notice that the muscles relax as you breathe out. Next, work on your muscles in a certain order from the top of your head to your feet. Relaxing your body physically can prevent you from becoming agitated.

3. Intense exercise

Do some intense workouts, even if it's for a short time. Intense exercises will help your body get rid of negative energy that usually comes from strong emotions you have bottled in. For example, you can run short or long distances, jog from one street to another, walk at a fast pace, do jumping jacks, or even swim. As you exercise, your body releases some endorphins, which help to deal with problematic emotions like sadness, anger, and anxiety.

In the next chapter, we will look at another helpful DBT tool called emotional regulation. Now, let's get right into it!

5

TOOL #3—THE WORLD OF EMOTIONAL REGULATION

> *"This might surprise you, but one of the best ways to manage your emotions is simply to experience that emotion and let it run its course."*

— KIM L. GRATZ

You may have heard the popular saying that change is the only constant thing in life. Indeed, change happens to every teenager, but positive change is usually driven by hope. So despite how severe your OCD is, you can still improve.

Now, before we go deeper into this chapter's message, let me share a story with you. This true life story is based on a woman's journey from OCD to healing.

When Wendy Mueller had her first child, she developed severe OCD symptoms that frustrated her mentally and emotionally. Like most people dealing with OCD, Wendy's OCD symptoms didn't start gradually or build over the months. Instead, they started overnight.

At the onset, Wendy battled intrusive thoughts and other OCD symptoms, often sinking her mood into a dark mental pit. Unfortunately, these feelings continued for two years, and eventually, she feared she was going crazy. When Wendy woke most mornings, she wondered why her head was always over-whelmed with obsessive thoughts and repetitive rituals, like checking her locks, placing things in perfect order, and constantly worrying about her newborn. Plus, she was nearly going paranoid that she might harm her baby.

Since Wendy hadn't heard about OCD, Wendy hid her symp-toms from everyone because she thought she was going insane and didn't want to be put in a mental ward. However, she went through treatment for her postpartum depression. Still, she refused to tell the psychiatrist that she had OCD symptoms. And, because she couldn't share her situation with others, she had to endure her suffering alone and in silence.

But a year after struggling with intrusive thoughts, Wendy found a 1989 issue of *Newsweek* magazine and read an article about OCD. The article detailed the journey of another woman dealing with OCD called Patricia Perkins, and it helped Wendy understand what she was really suffering from. As Wendy read the article, she learned Perkins was the founder of what was then called the Obsessive-Compulsive Foundation, now called the IOCDF. Fortunately, the article contained the foundation's contact information, so she immediately contacted them to ask if they had any OCD support groups in her area—and they did!

In her first meeting, she met about 15 people with similar experiences, which shocked her but also helped her realize that she wasn't alone. So, for the first time, Wendy could meet and talk to people who knew exactly what she was going through. She felt a huge weight lifted off her when she realized that everyone in the group understood what she was going through.

So, with time, she got on the right medication and learned exposure and response prevention techniques, which helped her resist her compulsions. In her own words, the results she got were miraculous after this. Eventually, Wendy progressed from being unable to do the things she loved due to OCD to recovering from OCD each day.

One of the most encouraging things about Wendy's story is all through those dark moments, she never thought happiness and peace would ever become part of her life again. But today, she has been free from OCD for over 20 years and is grateful for her journey to healing. Unfortunately, she has had to endure seeing her life as a horrible existence for so many years and is still working on stopping those intrusive thoughts from overwhelming her.

Although Wendy still gets certain OCD urges, she has come to accept that her journey so far has been significantly promising. And leaving the horrible, disabling anxiety of being controlled by OCD was a huge victory she'll always be proud of. Now, when she locks her door, she never feels the urge to recheck it anymore. She may read a paragraph twice but hardly ever more than that. Basically, whenever she refuses to submit to an OCD compulsion, she weakens her OCD.

So, I do hope her journey encourages you. No matter how OCD may affect your life, there is enough proof that you can go from deep OCD to recovery. Some teenagers go for exposure and response prevention therapies, while others focus on medication or both. In Wendy's case, she did both.

But let's focus on one technique to help set you on that journey toward recovery.

THE EMOTIONAL REGULATION OVERVIEW

Emotional regulation is a DBT skill that can help you understand your emotions better. It mostly focuses on factors like what motivates your emotions, why you express them the way you do, and the action urge that comes with every emotion you feel. Through emotional regulation, you will also learn to tell whether or not you must comply with these urges. This will help you reduce your vulnerability, increase your resilience against negative emotions, and boost your mental well-being.

So why do we call emotional regulation a DBT skill? It's simple. DBT skills help you manage your emotions better while responding to distress, and emotional regulation is helpful for people struggling with self-harm and other self-destructive behaviors.

Now, why should emotional regulation matter to you? Well, for one, emotional regulation is a DBT skill that will help you understand your emotions better, reduce your vulnerability to your feelings, and decrease emotional suffering. An essential part of emotional regulation is understanding that negative emotions aren't necessarily bad or something you must avoid. After all, they are a normal part of]every teen's life. However, there are some ways you can acknowledge them and eventually release these feelings so that they don't have full control of you.

Most teenagers with sensitive and extreme emotions go through emotional cycles that trigger negative thoughts automatically. Sadly, you can respond to these thoughts negatively, leading to harmful behaviors or decisions. For example, in my earlier story, Wendy sank into a pit of negative thoughts that worsened her mood and made her feel she was going crazy because she unknowingly nurtured these thoughts and allowed them to fester. And do you know what's worse? After these destructive behaviors, more negative emotions follow. For example, you may feel ashamed or start hating yourself.

The next question is this: why is emotional regulation necessary for OCD? For starters, emotional regulation will enhance the quality of your life, your emotional and physical health, your academic performance, and your relationships with your friends and family. In addition, emotional regulation will teach you to control your emotions through critical thinking and assessment of a situation or problem. This way, the chances of your negative emotions worsening and leading you into more trouble will reduce. Let me also add that emotional regulation can improve your mood. And once your mood improves, your ability to feel empathy and compassion for others will increase.

As a teen, you need to manage your emotions wisely so you do not encounter serious problems later in life. Hence, you need to learn and practice emotional regulation skills early.

Now that we've covered the basics of emotional regulation, let's look at some of its pros and cons.

✛ THE PROS OF EMOTIONAL REGULATION

First, let's begin with the pros:

1. Constructive communication

This is one of the best pros you will find here, and let me explain why. The fact is that teenagers—and even adults—who communicate through negative or destructive words or actions often have a destructive force behind them. You might think this is about yelling or screaming. But although yelling and screaming can be part of it, it goes beyond these actions.

For instance, if you have low self-esteem and feel you aren't good enough, you'll struggle to communicate your needs and desires well. And sadly, this will lead to conflicts with people you care about. You know why? Most people will be unable to tell how you are feeling or what you are thinning and so they too might get the wrong impression about you. Some might call you snobbish, rude, or unkind because your body language gave them that impression. Meanwhile, on the contrary, you are being held back by the feeling of not being good enough. But when you regulate your emotions, your listening will improve, and you can express yourself the right way. Also, you will be able to manage your emotions and function well from a place of peace instead of chaos.

2. Healthy choices

Teenagers are more prone to making bad decisions than most people of all ages and in all social groups. And they usually make these bad choices when they feel vulnerable or emotionally unstable. Trust me; I was no different. For instance, as a teenager, I ate more sugar whenever I started to feel bad about myself. Some teens use food to cope with stress, as I did. However, others turn to alcohol and drugs once they start feeling stressed. So whether it relates to food, recreational activities, or relationship with the opposite sex, teens generally make unhealthy choices while going through painful moments. But emotional regulation can help you manage your emotions better and make smarter decisions.

3. Peace-filled relationships

This is also related to the constructive communication I mentioned earlier. When you regulate your emotions, you'll be able to communicate with your loved ones from a place of peace. What's more, you will learn to show empathy and care while communicating with others. And you know the best? Being more empathetic to your friends shows them that you're on the same team, even when you don't tell them openly. This, particularly, will benefit you when you relate with schoolmates, meet new people, or interact with other teenagers.

You're more likely to make sarcastic comments to people close to you whenever you feel they didn't meet your needs or expectations. You can also say harsh things when you feel neglected or withdraw from your loved ones when they say things that hurt you. However, you'll be more deliberately vulnerable whenever you regulate your emotions, making you more confident to share your real feelings.

4. Intentional decisions

When you regulate your emotions, you will learn to accept the feelings raging inside you, especially when facing conflicts. Take a minute to think of how you'd react when you return home to an annoying sibling after a difficult day at school. You might probably direct your frustrations at them. Of course, this isn't a healthy response, but it sure does happen. And most times, you eventually realize that you have little control over outcomes like that.

Nevertheless, emotional regulation will help you make more intentional decisions. Life doesn't have to always control you, and you don't have to always feel like you aren't in control of what's happening around you. But with emotional regulation, you can make smart, intentional decisions starting today. You can also learn never to allow your emotions to tell you what to do or when to do it.

5. Self-esteem and self-confidence

At some point in our lives, we've all thought we weren't good enough to do, be, or achieve something. This feeling of inadequacy happens to everyone at some point. You might have said something similar to yourself in the past or even recently. For example, you could have felt you don't matter, especially after seeing people treat you like garbage. Or you might feel like you don't fit in.

Inadequacy and impostor syndrome are common among teenagers, but it worsens when you're dealing with OCD. You will usually feel like the abnormal one in the pack when that happens. But then, none of these thoughts are true.

Once you are emotionally regulated, it will be easier for you to focus more on the positive things about yourself that are true. You will also learn to accept your weaknesses with enough grace, just like others. In addition, you will learn to recognize and value your strengths.

6. Optimism and improved mood

Once you learn to regulate your emotions, you will be more optimistic. Your difficult moments won't make you feel so emotionally drained and moody. And even when you get moody or feel mentally low, you will easily bounce back. In other words, emotional regulation will make you more resilient to strong emotions, including anger and anxiety. Therefore, you will experience greater optimism and better moods once you practice emotional regulation.

— THE CONS OF EMOTIONAL REGULATION

1. Depression

One thing you might experience when you go through the emotional regulation process is depression. Because you'll be exposed to many negative emotions, you might find it difficult to manage them as you should. However, this can also be avoided once you follow a suitable emotional regulation training method such as guided meditation, breathing exercises, and mindfulness.

2. Lack of optimism

One of the challenges with trying something new is the hope or expectations that come with it. So, your optimism might fall if you aren't getting the expected results. As a result, you might lose faith in your ability to heal or become better.

3. Indecisiveness

Most teenagers fall into the trap of indecisiveness at some point in their lives. When you are feeling too many emotions, you can often become confused. For example, while trying to act in control instead of out of control, you could become uncertain about what action would be the best to take, leading to indecisiveness and more confusion and emotional pain.

4. Mood swings

Like indecisiveness, mood swings can also come from spending too much time in your head trying to make the right choice. Mood swings can happen to everyone, but while practicing emotional regulation, you could experience this as an aftereffect if done improperly.

THE SKILLS OF EMOTIONAL REGULATION

1. Recognizing your emotion

The first and most important skill of emotional regulation is to recognize your feelings. But before you can recognize an emotion, you need to be aware of it. So you need to observe your emotions and how you respond to them. And you can start by observing your body and determine where these emotional sensations are coming from. For example, is your heart beating fast? Do you notice any tension around your head or neck? These physical signs may be clues to the type of emotional experiences you are having. Once you start trying to find out what you might be experiencing physically, you will be able to switch your attention from dwelling on the physical pain to focusing on relieving yourself of some mental stress.

2. Being effective

Emotional regulation skills will help you to be more effective. The fear that comes from feeling inadequate will reduce, and you will be able to play and function better in school.

3. Emotional and physical vulnerability

You will also learn to be less emotionally and physically vulnerable because you will be well equipped to manage your feelings. Once you become a master of your own emotions, you will no longer be at the mercy of external or internal emotional triggers.

4. Self-exposure

Instead of avoiding or suppressing your emotions, you will learn to adapt and seek better ways to deal with them. This will guarantee long-term well-being and a permanent solution to your emotional distress. Also, self-exposure will teach you to shift your focus from the problem and lower the impact of your negative feelings through self-appraisal.

5. Self-validation

Self-validation is another way to build your emotional regulation skill. Here, you learn to set aside time for yourself every day to remind yourself that you have talents, gifts, and virtues. This skill is about allowing your mind to get to a flexible and relaxed state, which will change how you feel and respond to your emotions. Examples of self-validation hacks include the following:

- Daily positive self-affirmations
- Breath-control and relaxation techniques
- Meditation and compassion exercise
- Self-care routines
- Gratitude and journaling

6. Mastery and coping ahead

One thing about emotional regulation is that it makes you adapt more easily to situations and achieve the level of mastery you need to cope with difficult situations. However, an emotional imbalance will reduce your ability to adapt to changes in your life, whether they are positive or negative. As a result, you will be easily affected by distractions, and your coping mechanisms will weaken. This is why we resist changes in our lives. Meanwhile, an objective evaluation will help you build coping mechanisms.

For instance, if you are in a situation where stressful emotions seem to be bogging you down, your reactions to them might be destructive. First, you must take a pause. Then, take a moment to imagine that someone you care about, like your sibling or friend, was going through the same experience. Which solution would you suggest in such a situation? Write down your answer, then ask yourself if you are following your own advice.

EMOTIONAL REGULATION WORKSHEETS

"How Big Is My Problem?"

Let's try an exercise titled "How big is my problem?" This exercise is all about determining how big your problems are and rating them accordingly. Most of us tend to exaggerate our problems or, as is often said, "make mountains out of molehills." If this is an issue with you, the picture showing a list of emotions above can help you.

Below is a list of five levels a problem can potentially get to. Now, look at the list below and decide how you want to rate your problem or which level your problem falls under. What level do you fall under based on the emotions listed below? We begin with the most serious to the least severe.

Level 5: Emergency (e.g., danger, peril, fire, severe injury)

- **Potential emotions you may feel:** fear, panic, rage, frustration

Level 4: Huge problem (e.g., getting into a fight, getting lost, someone getting hurt)

- **Potential emotions you may feel:** Disappointment, fear, rage, anxiety

Level 3: Medium problem (e.g., experiencing a minor accident, facing disrespect, feeling sick)

- **Potential emotions you may feel:** worried, frustrated, exhausted, hurt.

Level 2: Small problem (e.g., forgetting to do your homework, confused about what to do, losing your supplies)

- **Potential emotions you may feel:** Unhappiness, disappointment, embarrassment, and annoyance

Level 1: Glitch (e.g., losing a game, being late for class, having your requests declined)

- **Potential emotions you may feel:** Contentment, passiveness, and calmness

The Cooldown Arena

The cooldown arena is an opportunity to find refuge whenever your emotions try to overwhelm you. This exercise is one effective way to practice emotional regulation skills. What's more, it will strengthen your relationship with your family, friends, and classmates. The cooldown arena is often a classroom, but you can set up your room to practice this activity.

First, the arena should be equipped with dim lighting, an mp3 player with calm and relaxing music, stress balls, markers, affirmation lists, papers, and scents such as strawberry and lavender. You can give your arena names such as "My Chill Zone" or "My Cool Spot."

To set up your arena properly, ask yourself these questions:

- What would you like to have in the cooldown area to make you feel happier, calmer, and safer?
- What community rules will you establish for yourself here to make you feel safe?

You can use this as your safe spot when you feel out of control, but don't wait until you explode before enjoying its benefit.

The Positive Self-Talk

You will need a lot of mental energy and power to do self-talk. Also, you will need constant practice, but trust me; it is so worth it. Nevertheless, positive self-talk will help you improve your social and academic performance.

Here is how you can do it:

- Whenever you have a negative thought about yourself, replace it with positive affirmations such as "I'm amazing, no matter what others think, say, or do to me."

Remember that positive self-talk can become a habit if you consistently say these words to yourself, and your mindset will become more positive as a result.

6

TOOL #4—BYE-BYE INTRUSIVE THOUGHTS

"*Thoughts are only thoughts. They are not you. You do belong to yourself, even when your thoughts don't.*"

—JOHN GREEN

Breaking an Object Negative Self-Talk Embarassing Moment

Becoming Violent Being a Failure

Flashback to Bad Memories Hurting Yourself

This chapter will look at another tool to help you deal with your OCD and understand how intrusive thoughts affect you.

But first, let's start by looking at how intrusive thoughts can affect you negatively.

DANGERS OF INTRUSIVE THOUGHTS

Intrusive thoughts are unwanted thoughts that can invade and take control of your mind without warning. They are often repeated again and again and can affect you in the following ways:

1. They can impact your mental health

Intrusive thoughts can disturb you and cause great distress, leading to mental health issues or worsening already existing problems. For example, thoughts about a painful event from your past can resurrect the long-forgotten emotions from that event. Also, most teens with symptoms such as anxiety and depression will likely experience intrusive thoughts. And these intrusive thoughts may worsen their mental health conditions and make it difficult for them to heal.

2. They can worsen your OCD

As with other mental health conditions, intrusive thoughts can worsen your OCD and then become worse *because* of your OCD. These thoughts may constantly remind you of something you haven't done well or make you feel imperfect or inadequate. The result is that you will continuously keep checking yourself to find the imperfection. These could be thoughts about how you arrange your stuff, fuss over notes, and organize your bedroom. As these thoughts continue to make you see even the most perfect things as not perfect enough, your OCD symptoms could become worse.

3. They can lead to anxiety and depression

Now, when I say intrusive thoughts can worsen your anxiety or depression, I mean both as part of OCD and on their own. For instance, let's say you are diagnosed with chronic anxiety and not OCD; you will still experience intrusive thoughts in the beginning.

At first, you may hear negative voices in your head trying to remind you of why you are a failure for failing math or why your crush at school isn't giving you any attention. Then, these thoughts feed on other negative experiences around you to convince you that you are indeed the worst person on earth, which is why no one likes you. Finally, it gets to the point where you live with these thoughts, and they become your reality. Soon, you start to feel discouraged, sad, and emotionally vulnerable. Eventually, anxiety and depression set in and may worsen if you do nothing about it.

4. They can be upsetting and affect how you behave

Although intrusive thoughts might seem harmless at first, they can negatively affect your quality of life. They may also affect how you behave, especially how you interact with your classmates, friends, and family. These thoughts can make you think wrongly of others and how they see you. For example, saying hello without getting a response from a classmate who is lost in thought or probably having a bad day might make you feel that such a person is proud and doesn't seem interested in talking to you. As a result, you start to feel bad about yourself and get the wrong notion about them. Of course, these thoughts aren't true, but you chose to believe them because you don't know how to prove them wrong.

So, in short, intrusive thoughts can be quite upsetting. They can also worsen your OCD, leading to depression and anxiety, and impact your mental health.

INTRUSIVE THOUGHTS OVERVIEW

First, let's look at what intrusive thoughts really are. Intrusive thoughts are like weeds on a vegetable farm. They are the unwanted mental images, impulses, thoughts, or urges you experience spontaneously, and they are caused by external and internal stimuli (by the way, a stimulus is something that causes your body to act somehow). As I said earlier, these thoughts often but not always cause you distress.

Intrusive thoughts are most common among teenagers with obsessive-compulsive disorder, but why is this so? First, like OCD, it is hard to tell where intrusive thoughts come from. They are unpleasant and also unwanted. Sometimes these thoughts could be aggressive or sexual, or it could be a sudden worry or excessive thinking about a mistake you made.

Intrusive thoughts can be about one or all of these listed items:

- Contaminations from germs or infections
- Acts of violence, aggression, or bringing harm to others
- The anxious feeling from doubting that you might do something wrong

- Fear of being immoral or not meeting your religious expectations
- Fear of making mistakes or saying the wrong thing in public

So, it's common to find intrusive thoughts among OCD patients because there is a relationship between OCD and intrusive thoughts.. For instance, in OCD, intrusive thoughts lead to emotional suffering. This is caused by this simple fact—teens often try very hard to suppress thoughts they don't want (obsessions). Usually, this would lead them to observe a routine or repeat a particular action.

THE INS AND OUTS OF INTRUSIVE THOUGHTS

Next, let's look at what causes intrusive thoughts and what they lead to,

1. Anxiety

Anxiety can make you fear that your door isn't properly locked, even after you've checked it for the hundredth time. This obsession with your door may be because you fear someone breaking in and hurting you or stealing something from you. So you are worried that these thoughts will resurface if you do not check again. Anxiety is one of the leading causes of intrusive thoughts. Intrusive thoughts are often disturbing and embarrassing, so very few teens share them.

Teens with clinical anxiety, for instance, will most likely judge themselves harshly for their intrusive thoughts. They might conclude that these intrusive thoughts make them terrible and dangerous people. And as these negative thoughts are repeated, the situation becomes a cycle where these intrusive imaginations become stronger, and your anxiety worsens again.

When that happens, it will be harder to ignore or simply dismiss these thoughts and continue with your life. Instead, you might end up obsessing over the intrusive thoughts, which will only worsen your OCD.

2. Depression

Some of the main signs of depression are hopelessness, sadness, self-doubt, inadequacy, guilt, lack of energy, low appetite, and poor sleep. But as terrible as these signs are, they could easily get worse when negative thoughts flood your mind.

Depressed teenagers often find it hard to deal with overwhelming thoughts. And the more depressed you are, the more room you give to intrusive thoughts. Likewise, the more intrusive thoughts you allow to breed in your mind, the more severe your depression gets.

For example, you may feel inadequate because you think you aren't good enough for anyone. It could also be because you judge yourself as awful before even giving yourself a chance. So, you keep fueling your depression with thoughts like, "If I didn't make it before after trying so hard, I could never make it now. I'm simply not good enough." Does this sound familiar?

Most times, intrusive thoughts are the reason why teens struggle to sleep well. You may spend most nights going back and forth with a thought or feeling. And the moment you manage to put one to sleep, another more severe one rages until you can no longer deal with them, and you finally surrender your will to them. Walk with me here. The truth is you will find a way out of this because there will always be a light at the end of the tunnel.

3. Fear

Fear isn't just a feeling—it's also a thought. For example, imagine you are asked to do a presentation in front of the whole school where around 1,000 people, including parents, teachers, and students, will be present. It's normal to be nervous, but ask yourself what causes that fear.

If you check properly, your fear comes from thoughts like "I'm not up to this," or "People will laugh at me if I make a terrible mistake." Perhaps, your mind is filled with images of your classmates laughing at you, so as soon as you climb the podium, your fear triggers more thoughts. Then, you begin to fuss about everything, from your clothes to how you think you look or behave. And as these distract you, you might lose your confidence and then make the same mistakes you're scared of making.

4. Need for symmetry

The need for symmetry is one of the most recognized features of obsessive-compulsive disorder. Even though the media like to stereotype OCD people as often living a life of uniformity, such as always aligning items in a funny way, not all OCD patients have this problem. Still, it is definitely part of many OCD experiences. For instance, teens who have OCD-related exactness or symmetry will experience the following:

- Extreme anxiety that a bad thing will happen to them if the number of things in their houses or school is uneven. For example, the pencils on their desk, the books on their shelves, or the items in their locker must have an even number.
- Strong reaction to anything that isn't symmetrical. For example, seeing asymmetrical words they find on a page, shoelaces on shoes, or something else that doesn't appear to be correctly arranged. Usually, these strong reactions stem from a thought that has waxed strong in their minds.
- An overwhelming desire for things to become balanced. For instance, the need to hold a cup of tea using both hands and apply just the same amount of energy on each side of the cup. These behaviors are products of intrusive thoughts.

5. Orderliness

Excessive need for orderliness is another effect of intrusive thoughts. OCD orderliness, for example, can be the compulsive behavior people with OCD have to deal with. You might want to always arrange and rearrange physical or visual objects. And this type of OCD comes with the constant need to line up objects, fix them in different positions, and organize your belongings so that they feel perfectly right to you.

And as I mentioned earlier, this desire comes with anxiety and restlessness, especially when you struggle to achieve the exact type of orderliness you want. This behavior is sometimes linked to perfectionism, although they aren't always the same. Still, they're both born from not being satisfied with something. Usually, you'll feel like you need to do something to make things better.

Teens with orderliness linked to OCD are usually preoccupied with intrusive thoughts such as the need to always be tidy and organized; this drives them to act compulsively. Sometimes, these thoughts will force you to become cranky and anxious over the simplest things. For example, you may get worked up when you see a pair of shoes that isn't neatly arranged or a stack of books that isn't in the right order. So these constant thoughts invade your mind and make you rearrange things frequently until you get to the point of relief and satisfaction. For some people, these thoughts will compel them to become fixated on a particular pattern or use counting methods to display balance while arranging items.

On the other hand, others may prefer to stick to a specific position they are more familiar with. So if someone disturbs this pattern, you may get angry and all worked up.

INTRUSIVE THOUGHTS WORKSHEETS

Now, let's do a few exercises to help you deal with intrusive thoughts.

Disobey on Purpose

The first exercise is called "disobey on purpose." Of course, this might not seem very clear at first, so I'll explain how it works. First, get up if you're sitting and carry your phone, a book, or any item you can handle. Next, walk around the room slowly while holding this item. As you do this, read the following sentence several times to yourself loudly. Yes, you must read the sentence while walking around your room.

Are you set? Okay, let's get started.

Simply say, "I cannot move around this room."

Now, keep strolling as you repeat that statement. Walk five or six times while you say, "I cannot walk around this room." Then, sit down.

It's pretty easy, right? But when you do this, you're simply poking the eye of the dictator inside you—some people call this the domineering part, as our minds often think it has the solution to all our problems. And that's why it keeps suggesting solutions to problems, particularly your psychological pains, which hardly ever work.

This activity is one of the early discoveries made by researchers seeking solutions to the problem of intrusive thoughts. Although it seems like a crazy exercise, a team of Irish scientists recently proved that it could increase tolerance for experimentally induced pain by nearly 40%. During their research, people were willing to place their hands on a very hot plate for 40% longer after they could say one thing while they did the opposite. But, of course, the plate was hot enough to cause real pain but not hot enough to cause injury.

You should try a small demonstration that shows your mind's power over you is an illusion, and it will give you higher freedom to do more difficult things. Also, this can easily be built into your life. And you can practice it regularly. For example, even while writing this sentence, I am thinking, "I will not type this sentence!" Funny, right?

Thought Records

A thought record is an exercise that will help you apply logic to your mental processes. For example, you may be scared you will fail a math test you just submitted. As a result, you may spend most of your day obsessing over how your teacher must feel disappointed with your work or that your work must be really bad.

This thought cycle may lead to it becoming a reality. For example, by thinking that something will go wrong, you might eventually end up doing something that will make it a reality. For example, if you've convinced yourself that you're a disaster at math, you may put off doing your math homework till the last minute. And because you've not got enough time to do it properly, you do end up making a mess of it. Therefore, to have a better sense of control, balance, and coherence, you must make records of those intrusive thoughts that invade your mind. All you have to do is write down every negative thought that enters your mind. After that, try to work out its truth.

Look at this for a guide: "I know that everything I wrote in the test was wrong. But how do I know this? Is there any proof that this is true? Has my teacher brought out the result yet? What did I write that might be wrong?"

Identifying Intrusive Thoughts

Is it possible to tell when you are experiencing intrusive thoughts? Well, of course, it is. And here are some signs to look out for:

The thought occurs often for you: Intrusive thoughts are quite consistent in their presence in your mind. However, intrusive thoughts that invade your mind are not the same as your typical thoughts. Sometimes, they can be so violent or even strange.

The thought causes disturbance: Once a thought begins to disturb you, and you feel like pushing it out of your mind, then it is most likely an intrusive thought.

It is usually difficult to control: Because intrusive thoughts are often repetitive, they are hard to take off your mind. So the more you think about them, the more anxious you become. So, rather than fight your intrusive thoughts, learn to live with them. Then, as they emerge, use the following steps to deal with them:

- Identify it as an intrusive thought. Say to yourself, "This isn't how I think or feel, so it must be an intrusive thought." Or, "This isn't what I believe or how I think, so it isn't what I will do."
- Don't yield to the urge to fight with it. Instead, once an intrusive thought enters your mind, simply accept it. "Do not try to force it to go away." You may recognize this from the mindfulness exercises.
- Do not judge or condemn yourself. Remember that nothing is wrong with you, so don't assume otherwise simply because you have a disturbing thought. You need to always treat yourself with kindness and compassion.

Hierarchy of Concerns

As someone once said, intrusive thoughts are like smoke from a chimney—they're the heat of something burning inside you. Believe it or not, that flame inside you is made up of your unresolved problems that worsen over time. So here is an exercise for you to deal with this:

- First, you need to control the focus of your thoughts, feelings, and anguish. Next, clarify them by creating a hierarchy of your problems and concerns. This hierarchy is simply a scale of your concerns that goes from the lowest to the highest.
- Begin by writing down all your concerns. This is simply your way of visualizing every chaos you have buried inside.

- Create a hierarchy representing everything you may consider as minor problems, then end with the most frustrating of all the challenges.
- As you round off and reach a complete set, start doing a personal reflection on each point. Try to think rationally. As you do so, come up with your best solutions to each item in the hierarchy.

The next chapter of this practical guide will shed more light on interpersonal effectiveness, so anticipate!

7

TOOL #5—ACCESSING YOUR INTERPERSONAL EFFECTIVENESS

> *"People with OCD, including myself, realize that their seemingly uncontrollable behavior is irrational, but they feel unable to stop it."*

— ABHIJIT NASKAR

Do you know that many core symptoms of obsessive-compulsive personality disorder often lead to interpersonal challenges? For instance, some scientists researched a group of OCD patients and found that most struggled to display empathy skills. This means that OCD can affect your interpersonal skills and make it hard for you to build strong relationships with other people.

But what are interpersonal relationships? Well, interpersonal relationships are simply your relationship with people around you. To understand this better, let's look at what communication is. Communication is your ability to exchange your thoughts, ideas, feelings, and emotions with someone face-to-face or through a medium. This exchange could be verbal (talking) or nonverbal (listening or using gestures to pass a message without saying anything).

But one challenge OCD might bring to you is the ability to communicate effectively, whether verbally or nonverbally. And when a person can't communicate or relate with someone else effectively on an interpersonal level, it means they lack interpersonal effectiveness. Most times, it isn't their fault. Deep down, you'd probably want to go out more, be friendlier and chattier with people, show empathy, etc. But sadly, you are confined in a mental box, and you can't do much to change this —or can you?

Interpersonal effectiveness is a group of skills you can learn even when you haven't developed them yet. For example, no one is born with the ability or inability to communicate effectively and relate well with others. Instead, we learn communication as a skill and gain relationships through our efforts. But like every skill, we can lose what we learn by lack of practice or due to other circumstances beyond our control.

Interpersonal effectiveness skill has its core goals, and the first is to get people to respect your needs, whatever they are. It is also about getting them to do what you want. Below are some other goals of this skill:

- To help you express your opinions and ensure people take you seriously
- To strengthen your relationships with friends, family, and classmates
- To build new, satisfying, and fulfilling relationships
- Finally, interpersonal effectiveness helps you end toxic relationships

As I said earlier, we aren't born with interpersonal effectiveness skills. Instead, we learn them. And sometimes, we make mistakes while learning them. So, while you try to build new relationships, your emotions might come in your way of building healthy relationships, and you might fail initially. Other times, our ANT (automatic negative thoughts) toward ourselves may affect our ability to find and make new friends, maintain existing relationships, or even end toxic ones.

The next questions we should ask on this journey are, "Does interpersonal effectiveness relate to DBT?" "And if it does, then how?" First, human relationships are like green plants. They need to be tender and full of juice to stay healthy. If such a plant grows to become a tree, it needs a healthy system of roots for nourishment and support. And the tree only grows bigger and stronger as its roots grow. This development also helps it produce tasty fruits with time.

Your relationships are like this tree, and each relationship you have with others has its roots. Therefore, the root must be healthy for you to grow a healthy relationship. Now, where am I heading with all this? Well, this is where the dialectical behavior therapy (DBT) relationship with interpersonal effectiveness begins. DBT gives you specific skills to develop strong roots, and these strong roots will help you build and maintain healthy, fruitful, and rewarding relationships. Teens who have experienced healthy relationships throughout their lives develop these skills easily. So no matter how bad your case is, if you can master these skills, you will learn how to deal with your OCD better, especially by improving your relationships.

THE INS AND OUTS OF INTERPERSONAL EFFECTIVENESS

Next, let's look at the benefits and challenges of interpersonal relationships.

Benefits

1. Less loneliness

Interpersonal communication helps improve your relationship with people around you. One reason people often stay away from us is that they may feel unwanted, or we may be giving off a nonverbal message that says, "I don't need you." And when people feel unwanted, they will stay away because they don't want to be a burden to us. However, you will attract more people to you when you learn to improve your verbal and nonverbal communication skills. Also, more people will enjoy being around you, which will help you build healthy relationships and feel less lonely.

2. Having the knowledge that someone cares

Interpersonal effectiveness lets you know someone cares about you, and this can improve your sense of belief and hope—two things you need to help you through your healing journey. When you can give positive energy and receive positive energy from others, it gives you joy and comfort. You get to feel that you matter in their world and that they matter in yours. So as you spend time building healthy relationships with people, you are applying interpersonal effectiveness skills that will encourage your mind to accept that someone cares about you. And this knowledge will help you build hope and trust in the long run.

3. Optimism

One thing a healthy relationship does for you is to fill you with optimism. Healthy relationships give you hope that there is always someone to trust and confide in. What's more, they assure you that you won't be judged because of who you are or your condition. Also, because interpersonal effectiveness skills help build healthy relationships, you will become more confident about your ability to make new friends. As a result, you'll rarely feel out of place among strangers.

4. Self-esteem

Interpersonal effectiveness will also help you improve your self-esteem. Naturally, developing relationships and communicating effectively with teens and adults around you will improve your sense of worth. It will also make you feel that you are valuable to the people in your life. And people will become more comfortable sharing their pains, making you feel needed.

5. Less pain

One of the major causes of emotional and mental distress is the feeling of being alone, unloved, or uncared for. But fortunately, it will help you develop relationships that will get rid of these feelings. Talking to people in your life can affect you more positively than being alone with your thoughts and feelings. Likewise, sharing your emotions with your loved ones can help reduce your pain. So whether you communicate verbally or simply hang out with close friends, you are building a unique coping mechanism for the tough moments in your life.

6. Stimulation

Interpersonal effectiveness stimulates skills that will encourage you to be more human and accepting of others. For example, love, empathy, and kindness are important attributes of interpersonal communication, and interpersonal effectiveness will stimulate you to possess these attributes. Better yet, maintaining these attributes will endear more people to you.

Challenges

1. Dissatisfaction

Interpersonal effectiveness means you must learn skills to draw people closer to you, relate better with them, and win new friends. However, if your expectations for people are too high, you might struggle to be satisfied with their company, which can make you keep to yourself. When you try to build a relationship, and your expectations are dashed, it's normal to feel disappointed.

2. Inability to listen to others

One of the challenges you might face when meeting people is that you may struggle to listen to or appreciate their opinions. Although it is always good to understand other people's perspectives, most of us get to that point where we feel only our opinions matter, which isn't true. Other people's views matter too. And part of interpersonal effectiveness skills is to teach you to understand and accept this. However, the challenge of coming in contact with and listening to people is this: we may often behave in certain ways that make it difficult for them to listen to us, or they might act in certain ways that make it difficult for us to listen to them.

3. Lack of transparency and trust

One of the major challenges of human relationships is the lack of transparency and trust. Not everyone is comfortable with the truth, and very few teenagers are open to saying or hearing the truth. Then again, no one can really blame them. You see, some teenagers mistake judgment for truth, so instead of helping matters, they make the situation worse with the words they say to others.

On the other hand, there is a group of teens you might find difficult to trust. After confiding in them, they use your troubles as a weapon to mock you behind your back or even to your face. The final group is those who are hardly open to you. It may be tough to tell what their motives or intentions are, as they aren't transparent, which can make it nearly impossible to trust them.

4. Conflicts

In every relationship, conflicts are bound to occur. It is almost impossible to avoid it. For example, there might be a conflict of interest when you don't agree on the same thing with your friends or classmates or have little fights with your siblings. Some disputes can be mild, while others can last for years. Therefore, as long as we are open to meeting people, we must understand that conflicts may arise for one reason or the other. You should also be open about addressing those conflicts with your partner or friend when it arises because it is a sign that you have good conflict resolution skills.

THE SKILLS OF INTERPERSONAL EFFECTIVENESS

As humans, relationships are at the core of our existence. Whether it is relationships with our parents, guardians, friends, or classmates, we all need them to thrive. For some reason, we need to connect to people to find meaning in our existence. Believe it or not, our relationships give us a sense of purpose. So you must discover your identity and build self-sufficiency to become strong and dynamic as you grow into adulthood.

But this doesn't mean we don't need relationships because your emotional and physical connections with others are key to your development. So identifying and strengthening your interpersonal skills can bring you great happiness.

The best time to learn these skills is when you're a child, but it's not too late to develop them as a teenager. Usually, our parents and teachers are supposed to help us develop these skills by modeling them. But many teenagers today don't get the best teaching or parental models as a child, so they have to learn on their own. However, even if your childhood wasn't the most ideal, you still have the chance to make a more favorable choice for yourself.

Now that we've covered some pros and cons of interpersonal effectiveness, let's look at the specific skills you need to master interpersonal effectiveness.

1. Knowing what you want

When building relationships with people, defining what you want from the relationships is the first and most important thing to do. You need to know what you truly want from others. For instance, some people might make you uncomfortable when interacting with them because they don't meet your needs. However, others may give you a sense of security, which will make you open to them.

Then, there are those who make you feel comfortable and you've no idea why. When you find these people, it is important to find out what about them makes you feel comfortable and look for it in your new relationships. Your comfort and discomfort around people reveal your deepest interpersonal needs and desires.

2. Asking for what you want

Learn to express your needs to people—always be honest and transparent with them. One important lesson I have learned is this: When I open up about my needs in a relationship, especially when those needs are valid and not harmful, the relationship is always stronger and more fulfilling. So always be open to communicating your needs to people. Do you want a hug? Ask for it. Do you want them to take a walk in the park with you? Tell them.

But while you open up about your needs, always be polite and kind. Don't be judgmental, and don't make them feel terrible for not meeting your needs. I understand that sometimes, the fear of rejection can make you reluctant to express your needs to someone. But you can learn to be assertive, reinforce your needs, and stay mindful while you do so. Lastly, don't allow distractive thoughts such as unpleasant emotions (fear, anxiety, worry, jealousy, and anger) to distract you as you open up about your needs.

3. Negotiating conflicting wants

Conflict is inevitable in human relationships. Even our pets sometimes get upset with us, so what about humans with all our fire-filled emotions? Therefore, you must be willing to skillfully negotiate with people to resolve conflicts with them. And one way to do this is to realize and accept there aren't winners or losers.

When you argue, your goal should be to come to a position of compromise or acceptance. I often see verbal arguments as some sort of therapy, like an opportunity for the other person and me to let out the emotions raging inside us. Arguments are also an opportunity to build relationships and understand people better. They are not a chance to win a debate or find out who the villain or hero was.

In every relationship, one person may not always be right or wrong. Since we are all capable of making mistakes, each of us make mistakes. We just have to be understanding and listen to one another, and reach a point of negotiation where you are willing and ready to make compromises. This way, both your needs will be met. Also, you must learn to accept that you may not always get the result you want in every conflict.

4. Getting information

Other people's needs are just as valid as yours, so another important skill in interpersonal effectiveness is determining the needs, wishes, cares, and fears of those around you. However, there is no limit to the needs of others, so there is no limit to the amount of information you can seek regarding other people's needs. Sadly, we can be restricted from getting this key information when any of the following happens:

- We believe that we already know what other people want
- We impose our needs, wishes, fears, or desires on others

CALM THE CHAOS! OVERCOMING OCD FOR TEENAGERS | 133

- We worry that if we try too hard to get information about others' needs, they'll think we're prying
- We are worried about getting the worst possible response from them if we ask about their needs
- We might not be sure about what information to get from them.

5. Saying no correctly

Saying no to people isn't as easy as spelling the word itself. Particularly when you are attached to them, afraid of them, worried that they do not understand, offended by your reaction, or you might push them away. But any of these can happen depending on how you say "no" to them.

There are three ways you can say no to others. First, there is the flat or weak "no" that gives other people the chance to overpower you. Then, there is the brash or aggressive one that makes others avoid you. Finally, there is the "no" said in a powerful way that considers others' needs and desires and sets a clear boundary regarding what you want or don't want. Of all three styles, the third one is the one you should use in your relationships.

6. Acting according to your values

It is important to act according to your values. But when we behave passively or aggressively in our relationships, we simply deny the other person and ourselves the opportunity to have a healthy relationship. Therefore, the first step to acting according to your values in a relationship is to define those values.

Ask yourself the following questions and answer them honestly: "What type of connection do I want to build?" "And what type of relationships do I really want from others?"

You could also try to find out what a trusting, caring, or loving relationship means to you; this will help you understand what you truly want. As a teenager, you must learn to define your values and infuse these values into your old and new relationships. But how can you do this? Well, it's easy. Simply tell people what you value in a relationship. For example, tell them "I value your time," "I like that you always pay attention when I talk to you," or "You are so patient with me." Sometimes, show them and not just tell them. That is, let them know the things you value in them and act according to those values. If you appreciate their listening ability, you must also be a good listener to them.

THE INTERPERSONAL EFFECTIVENESS WORKSHEETS

No Listening Activity

Although this is a group activity, you can practice it with your friends or colleagues. This is simply an acting (role-playing) activity.

First, break the group into pairs before you start the activity. So, in each group, one person is asked to speak while another listens. After this, let them switch roles so that the person who first spoke now has to listen, and the person who first listened now has to speak.

So, each person takes 2 minutes to talk about any topic that interests them. For example, they could speak about sports, film, entertainment, school, life, politics, etc. So, while Partner A is speaking, Partner B has one job—they must try to make it look like they aren't listening to Partner A at all.

Partner B must not say anything; instead, they should rely on body language to send their message to Partner A. Once Partner A exhausts their two minutes, Partner B gets their own two minutes to talk, while Partner A now listens while pretending not to. In the end, you'll notice that each person struggled to keep talking when it seemed their partner wasn't listening.

The main message from this lesson is this: body language plays a vital role in communication. Also, listeners and speakers play major roles in how effective a conversation is.

After every group has had their turn to speak and listen, ask each person to write down how they felt when they thought their partners weren't listening to them. For example, they could write something like the following:

- I was annoyed.
- I became frustrated.
- It made me feel unimportant.
- I couldn't continue speaking.

Also, they should write down their partners' behavior that showed they weren't listening. For example, they could write

- looking away while I was talking;
- playing with their mobile devices;
- refusing to make eye contact;
- folding their arms;
- kept acting bored.

Sabotage Exercise

This exercise is quite fun. It uses poor interpersonal behaviors to show us what good interpersonal behaviors look like.

You will need a fairly large group to practice this exercise. Generally, this group should be such that you can easily split yourselves into two or three groups containing four or five participants.

The first instruction for each group is to take 10 minutes to brainstorm, list, and discuss the different ways they can disrupt a group assignment. They can think of anything as long as it is effective enough to sabotage a group task and probably rile the group.

Once each group has successfully come up with a way to sabotage a group task, you should all gather into the larger group again. As soon as everyone has regrouped, compare the responses you have from each group, then write them down on a chalkboard, large cardboard, whiteboard, or Flipboard positioned in front of the room.

The next thing to do is to go back to your smaller groups and create a 5- to 10-point contract and guidelines you have all agreed upon for successful group work. Then, each group member should draw from the ideas you came up with to sabotage group assignments.

For example, suppose a group states, "ignore other group members" as their tactic to sabotage the assignment. In that case, you can come up with something like, "listen to the other group members when they communicate with you." This will therefore be their tactic for successful group work.

This activity will help you learn what and what not to do during a group activity.

Counting the Squares

This fun and engaging game will encourage you to interact with one another when you are in a group. To play it, you need an image containing forty squares, or similar images, displayed on a whiteboard, PowerPoint, or anything everyone can see. Place this image in front of the room.

The first step is to instruct each player to count the number of squares displayed and write down their answer. But they should do this without talking to anyone.

Next, each group member should call out the number of squares they counted. Once they have done this, write their answer on the board.

Afterward, each participant should pair with someone and count the squares. They can discuss ONLY with their partner when counting the number of squares. Then, once they are done, each pair can share their answers with the entire group.

Next, each participant must form groups of four to five members and count the squares once more. Once they come up with an answer, write down the numbers each group has counted.

In the end, one group must at least have the correct answer, which is 40. Whichever group wins should tell the rest how they came up with the correct answer.

Finally, discuss why the count kept getting closer to 40 as more people got together to tackle the challenge.

Nonverbal Introduction Game

First, this game can be planned on the first day whenever a new group gets together for the first time, a training session, or any other activity that allows you to introduce each person in the group.

First, each group member should pair up with someone sitting next to them. Then, they should introduce themselves and say something interesting about themselves to the other person.

Once that has been done, everyone should redirect their attention to the larger group. Each person should now introduce their partner to the larger group. However, the trick is this— they cannot use words or props. So, each person will introduce their partner using actions only.

This particular game is basically an icebreaker for introducing people in a group to one another. It is also a fun way to explore the importance of verbal and nonverbal communication.

In the next chapter, you will learn about the sixth and final tool for dealing with OCD. So stay tuned.

8

TOOL #6—DEALING WITH COMPULSIONS

"Your mental health is everything—prioritize it. Make the time like your life depends on it, because it does."

— MEL ROBBINS

Before you can understand what compulsions are, you must know how they differ from obsessions. I've already explained that obsessions are harmful, disturbing thoughts, including images and impulses that suddenly crawl into your mind. These thoughts cause sudden anxiety and distress to you. On the other hand, compulsions are deliberate behaviors such as washing hands and checking the door knob or mental acts such as praying, counting, and repeating phrases. These behaviors or actions are carried out to help you reduce the behavior the obsessions caused.

When dealing with OCD, your natural response is usually to fight the unwanted intrusive thoughts. And as I explained earlier, you will often do this using purposeful behaviors and intentional actions, like self-assurance and avoiding people, places, and objects.

In the first stage, some teenagers with OCD may not visibly experience obsessive fear but only compulsions. So, in this rare case, it is either the teen doesn't have OCD (OCD needs to include obsessions *and* compulsions), or they once had obsessive worry at first but forgot it over time. Now, the type of obsession they are experiencing is simply the feeling of discomfort that they have OCD.

In simple terms, compulsive acts or compulsions may be considered repetitive acts done deliberately. They are intentional physical or mental actions you are compelled to do and are purely based on your own strict rules.

Normally, you'd experience some form of resistance to these acts. However, your resistance will be overpowered by a strong or subjective drive to do the action. Usually, the main aim behind this compulsive behavior is to gain temporary relief from the anxiety caused by the particular obsession.

Compulsive behaviors involve performing actions repeatedly and following a structured and well-defined routine, and they are connected to your obsessions. So you may have this strong fear that you or your loved ones are in imminent danger if you don't deal with the compulsion.

Do you notice that your compulsions are often irrational? Well, you are not alone. Many teens with OCD deal with this feeling as well. And even though they know their compulsions are irrational, they still feel bound to do them.

Teenagers living with OCD often experience a strong sense of responsibility to perform any behavior that can help them neutralize harmful thoughts. They'd likely hope that they can prevent themselves from being harmed by doing so. Sometimes, you may want to engage in that behavior to help you feel right, satisfied, or comfortable.

An example of this behavior is a common and well-known stereotype that OCD compulsion involves washing one's hands due to a compulsive fear that one might get a disease or get contaminated. For instance, many people without a disease will wash their hands and notice that their hands are dirty. But someone with OCD who has contamination as their obsessions would usually feel that their hands are messy and keep washing until they feel clean. Your OCD is simply telling you to continue that ritual because it is the only way you can keep yourself and your family safe. Therefore, this increased feeling of responsibility and the need to protect your loved ones keeps driving you to repeat the endless ritualistic behaviors.

It is important to deal with your compulsions as soon as possible. If you don't address them immediately, they may develop into more severe symptoms, making it harder for you to cope. If you have an OCD symptom, talk to a mental health professional for help. A therapist will guide you to identify obsessions and compulsions. They will help you start the process of dealing with them to reduce the impact they have on you.

TYPES OF OCD COMPULSIONS

1. Mental compulsions

The first type of compulsion is mental ones, which come in different ways. First, a mental compulsion could be some level of reassurance in recalling a particular incident, event, or situation from the past or present. For example, the mental thought could be that you think you have misbehaved at one point in the past. You also experience mental compulsions when you repeatedly check switches, boxes, locks, and body reactions. In this case, the obsessive thought may be that you're worried about an imminent danger and want to prevent it. Therefore, while mental compulsions are the things you do because of the fears, worries, anxiety, or pain in your mind, obsessive thoughts are the things you think about. Usually, they are the things you think about, but when you act upon them consistently, then they become compulsions.

In addition, they could also mean checking items over and over to see if they are arranged correctly. Your obsessive thought might be that something bad may happen if they aren't aligned. So, in summary, mental compulsions include:

- mentally reviewing events to prevent harm to yourself or others or avoid terrible consequences;
- praying to prevent terrible consequences or harm to yourself and others;
- counting while performing a task so that you end on a safe, good number, or right number, which is usually just an even number; and
- constantly canceling or undoing things; for example, replacing a "bad" or negative word with a "good" word.

2. Cleaning and washing compulsions

Cleaning and washing compulsions consist of constantly washing your hands excessively or in a particular way. You probably are afraid that if you don't wash your hands that way, you or someone close to you might become contaminated by a disease or a virus, even though there is no proof to guarantee that yet.

It also includes excessive showering, bathing, brushing teeth, grooming, or other toilet routines. This compulsion happens because you are afraid of imminent danger around you. What's more, your compulsions can include frequently cleaning household items or objects, while your obsession might be the fear of falling sick because of contamination.

It may also include doing other things that help remove or prevent contact with germs. For example, avoiding physical contact, refusing to shake others' hands, or immediately dusting off parts of your clothes or body when they make contact with another person.

When dealing with these compulsions, you might ask yourself questions like, "What if I contract a virus by not washing my hands?" "What if I spread germs on my friends and loved ones and they fall ill?" These questions could then lead the further compulsions like the ones below:

- Washing hands, body, and clothes excessively
- Bathing, showering and grooming excessively
- Cleaning objects, furniture, appliances, and parts of the house excessively

3. Repetition compulsions

You can describe repetition compulsions as a psychological phenomenon where you simply repeat an event or the situations that happened in that event repeatedly. Sometimes, it might include reliving these situations or putting yourself in similar situations. People with OCD may also relive these experiences in their dreams. When this happens, their memories and feelings are simply repeated in their dreams and imaginations. Sometimes, the reliving experience happens through hallucinations, too.

So, we can also simply say that repetition compulsions describe a pattern where people endlessly repeat unpleasant or distressing behavior patterns.

What's more, repetitive compulsions can be done mentally or physically, but most importantly, they are repetitive. And this is what sets them apart from other types of compulsions. For example, you might reread an email, text message, or internet page time and again to ensure you didn't miss anything. Another example is repeatedly rewriting a paragraph until you feel it's perfect.

Other common examples of repetition compulsions include the following:

- Saying the same thing over and over again
- Overanalyzing things repeatedly
- Repeating or reenacting routine activities, such as climbing up and down the stairs or getting off and on a chair
- Rereading a single text in a book repeatedly
- Repeating some types of body movements, such as blinking
- Doing a certain task or activity repeatedly several times
- Making excessive corrections on something you have written

4. Arranging and reordering compulsions

This compulsion happens due to the discomfort you feel when you see objects set in a way that doesn't suit you. Even if these items are arranged or in order, as long as they aren't arranged or ordered to your taste, you will feel unsatisfied and uncomfortable about it. You might also feel anxious if you walk into your class and find that the books on the class bookshelves or the papers on your desks are not aligned symmetrically. You might also feel uncomfortable that other objects such as chairs and tables do not have a certain distance between them. Sometimes, you might color-code pencils and paper clips to derive some relief.

Teens who deal with these compulsions might often feel they need to arrange objects in a certain way or several times before they can *really* be satisfied. They might also incorporate a special pattern into their routine while arranging items. For example, some teens may engage in counting mentally. They might also be slow to complete their daily tasks because their belongings must be set in a certain position or place.

So, if you find yourself taking time to set the table or tidy the house, well, now, you know why. Don't be surprised if you become furious or distressed when others move things slightly from where you had placed them. All these are common expressions of arranging and reordering compulsions.

THE COMPULSION EXERCISES

There are several exercises to help you deal with compulsions. But here, we will deal with the three most effective exercises.

Progressive Relaxation

This exercise is also called progressive muscle relaxation (PMR), and you can use it with the breathing activity we did in previous chapters. You can also use PMR to identify hidden tension around your body.

Here is how you can practice PMR. First, sit or lie comfortably in a quiet room, then start doing a breathing exercise. As you inhale, clench all the muscles in your face, then hold this breath for around 10 to 20 seconds and move down your body gradually—clenching your muscles in other parts. Movement should go around your shoulders, arms, stomach, buttocks, calves, and legs repeatedly. It's crucial that you repeat this inhalation pattern.

Interactive Metronome

I know this sounds new, so let me first explain. First, it should be done under the supervision of a healthcare professional. An interactive metronome is a type of therapy frequently used by professionals in healthcare to help patients improve their sensory integration. It is a state-of-the-art technology that keeps your body and brain in sync, which is essential for them to work in perfect harmony.

This exercise is a training tool that can significantly improve your sensory integration processes, and we'll soon explore how it works.

Generally, the interactive metronome is a process that organizes your environment, body, and mind's ability to feel and think. When this happens, it will become easier for you to use your body effectively within your environment. It is a technological device that works within what scientists call "the neural-timing network" and the dorsolateral prefrontal cortex, cerebellum, basal ganglia, and cingulate gyrus. These areas of your brain are being integrated. Yes, these are complex. But all that means is that the interactive metronome is a technological device that improves your brain's function and your body's performance within your environment (in class, study, play, walking in nature, activity at home, etc.).

When using the interactive metronome to perform exercises, you will need headphones, a computer screen, and a set rhythm. When you get all these, try to perform your exercises while in rhythm with a specific beat. You will find this device majorly in a clinic where it has already been set up for you to use. As you do this, this advanced technology will help you combine sound, timing, coordination, and other exciting things. It will also provide feedback on your result, which your therapist will use to track your movements and help you reach your desired goals.

A clinic is the best place and environment to do this. You may decide to set the metronome at different tempos, allowing a healthcare professional to increase the speed or slow down the connections.

Finally, remember that the interactive metronome is goal-oriented, well-structured, and designed to encourage you to perform motor movements. And these motor movements are repetitive, synchronized, and customizable to a specific reference tone. Your healthcare professional will also get audio and visual feedback to assess you, which are measured in milliseconds to improve the rhythm and timing.

Physical Activity

Daily exercises can help you optimize both your mind and body's health. However, there are many options but very little information regarding the type of physical activities you can engage in, which can be overwhelming. So let's look at three physical activities that can benefit you.

- **Lunges**

This activity will help you challenge your balance, which is an essential part of a complete exercise routine. Lunges help to improve functional movement and strengthen your legs and glutes.

Here is how you can make lunges;

1. Begin by standing on your feet, then broaden your shoulders (make sure they're level and not slouching) and allow your arms to lean or hang down loosely at both sides of your body.
2. Next, take a forward step with your right leg, then bend your right knee while you do so. Make sure you stop when your thigh is parallel to the ground and that you don't extend your right knee beyond the right foot.
3. Thirdly, push up from your right foot, then return to your starting position. Now repeat this process by putting your left leg forward. This is a single rep.
4. Finally, complete three sets of ten reps.

- **Squats**

This second physical exercise will help you improve your lower body and core strength and the flexibility around your lower back and hips. This activity engages the largest muscles in your body, so they pack a serious punch when it comes to burning calories.

1. Begin with your feet positioned a little wider than both shoulders. Place your arms on both sides.
2. Next, brace your core. While raising and maintaining a higher chin and chest, push your hips back and then bend your knees as though you'll sit on a small stool.
3. After that, drop down until your thighs are at the same level (parallel to) as the ground, but make sure your knees don't bow inward or outward. At the same time, bring your arms into a comfortable position in front of you. Next, pause for a second, then follow this by stretching your legs and returning to the starting position.
4. Do three sets of twenty reps.

- **Burpees**

Although some teens find this exercise difficult, it is a super effective way to strengthen your cardiovascular endurance and muscle strength.

1. First, stand upright with your feet shoulder-width apart, then place your arms down at your sides.
2. Squat down with your hands out in front of you. As soon as your hands reach the ground, stretch your legs back into a pushup position.

3. Thirdly, jump your feet up to your arms by hinging at your waist. Make sure to get your feet as close to your hands as possible, then land them outside your hands if possible.

4. Stand up straight while you bring your arms over your head, then jump.

5. This is a single rep, so complete 3 sets of 10 reps for starters.

9

OCD FAQS

> "It's like you have two brains—a rational brain and an irrational brain. And they're constantly fighting."
>
> — EMILIE FORD

In this chapter, we'll cover some of the most frequently asked questions that teenagers have about OCD. So let's get right into it!

Question #1: What is the difference between obsessions and compulsions?

Although both compulsion and obsessions are linked with OCD and other mental health disorders, they are very different. For instance, when your mind is flooded with persistent thoughts, we refer to these as obsessions. So obsessions are thoughts that work in your mind persistently. On the other hand, compulsions are the actions that result from those thoughts.

A compulsion is that action you keep taking (persistent action) because of a strong urge to engage in it. This urge comes from a thought (obsession), and the action keeps repeating itself until it disrupts your daily life. So the main difference between the two is that obsession relates to thoughts, while compulsion relates to action.

Let me give you a more detailed picture of what the two concepts mean and how they are different. First, obsessions happen to everyone. They are thoughts, images, and impulses that wouldn't leave your mind no matter how hard you try. Imagine a stranger barging into your house every time without knocking, and each time you try to send them away, they just wouldn't leave. Later, other strangers join in, knowing full well that the others tried and succeeded in overpowering you. Then they mess up your house.

This is how obsessive thoughts are. They are intrusive, and your mind becomes soiled with their dirty footprints. Teens with obsessive thoughts often say that they aren't normal, so you see why they are like uninvited human strangers? Even the word "obsession" is from a Latin root word that means "to besiege" or "to occupy." Plus, these thoughts don't just stain your mind once they occupy it; they also leave you with excessive anxiety and distress.

Some common obsessions include fear of germs or harm, unwanted sexual thoughts, blasphemous impulses or images, or violent fantasies.

In contrast, compulsions are behaviors or mental acts you perform to help you manage your anxiety or distress. Sometimes, you may perform these actions to avoid a terrible situation or experience. Other times, you do them because they're simply rituals. Some examples include repeatedly washing your hands or clothes, checking to see if someone is at your window, praying, counting and reciting, touching or tapping repetitively, or constantly seeking reassurance.

Finally, both obsessions and compulsions can happen separately. However, they often occur together, and this makes them related. Compulsions are simply trying to control the anxiety you are experiencing because of the obsessions. But the sad truth is that when you perform those compulsions, you simply strengthen the obsession-compulsion cycle.

Question #2: How common are obsessions and compulsions?

Generally, obsessions and compulsions are very common. Researchers from Yale University did a study and found that 28% of people in the general population have obsessions and compulsions. Also, doctors only diagnose OCD when your obsessions and compulsions are frequent and severe enough to cause enough distress and affect your ability to function. Not all OCDs are diagnosable because they may not be so obvious. However, around 1.6–2.5% of the population have OCD that can be diagnosed. But, sadly, just a small portion of that number receive a diagnosis and treatment.

Some data show that around 1.2% of people over 18 years are affected by OCD yearly, which is equivalent to 1 in 100 people.

However, 1 in 50 people, at any given time, are affected by OCD,which amounts to 2.3% of the population.

Some researchers say that there is a higher chance of you developing OCD at a young age if you are born as a male child. But in some situations, people with OCD symptoms will more likely receive a diagnosis in their late teens, between 18 and 19 years.

Question #3: Do teens with OCD believe in irrational thoughts?

Teens suffering from OCD know that their compulsions and obsessions are irrational. In fact, knowing that their thoughts are irrational is part of the suffering they go through. However, their awareness of what these thoughts are doing to them doesn't really reduce the distress from the obsessions, nor does it make it easier for them to resist the compulsions.Instead, it makes them feel ashamed, embarrassed, and alone.

Also, the emotional parts of their brain make them feel like they or someone else has contaminated their hands with harmful germs. Sometimes, they feel like they might have knocked someone with their bicycle or hit them while walking in the hallway. These parts of their brain often assumes that they forgot to switch off the heater before leaving home, so they fear their house might burn down before they get home.

This distressing feeling usually doesn't end until they perform that compulsive act. For example, they are often compelled to repeatedly wash their hands with hand sanitizer within five minutes of the first wash. They could also go back and forth within a particular route they just took, looking for a pedestrian they might have knocked down with their bicycle. Or they could return home to see if they switched off the bathroom heater.

Question #4: Is OCD a mental illness?

OCD is linked with some brain abnormalities like hyperactivity. And people with OCD experience this abnormality in several brain regions, like the anterior thalamus, basal ganglia, the anterior cingulate cortex, and the orbitofrontal cortex. Although OCD can be called a brain disease, it can also be called a psychological condition because it affects your mind and is influenced by life experiences. So, yes, it is a mental illness.

Teens with OCD may do special psychotherapy or take medications, as they're both effective. However, medications may work better for some OCD patients and not for others.

Even today, psychiatrists still find the relationship between brain abnormalities and psychological symptoms quite mysterious. It is still unclear if one of them happens first—that is, if there is a profound abnormality in the brain because of genes, leading to OCD. Or do these obsessions and compulsions develop to reflect how your brain functions?

Or maybe it's a bit of both—there are underlying genetic and other biological factors that perhaps decide why someone is at more risk and another person developing OCD has lower stakes. Perhaps, their life experiences contribute to who eventually has a disorder and who does not. The possibilities are endless and baffling.

Question #5: What are the symptoms of OCD?

Anxiety is one of the major symptoms teens affected by OCD will experience. And as I stated earlier, teens with OCD experience obsessions and compulsions that interfere with everything they do. These obsessions include persistent impulses, ideas, or images that enter your mind uninvited, and their goal is to cause you anxiety and distress. For example, thoughts that make you feel you have germs or some form of contamination on your body are common obsessions. Others include repeatedly doubting yourself, a strong need to put things in order, constant sexual imagery, and violent impulses.

On the other hand, compulsions are your efforts to hide, neutralize, or prevent those thoughts from becoming a reality. And you do that by doing some rituals or repeated actions like washing your hands, repeatedly checking or rearranging items, or doing repetitive mental acts such as counting or repeating words.

Question #6: At what age does OCD begin?

There isn't an age limit for when OCD can begin, so it can start anytime. In fact, OCD can start from preschool and last up till your adulthood, although males experience it earlier than females. For instance, males' age of onset is between the ages of 6 and 15, and females, between 20 and 29 years.

Question #7: Is OCD inherited?

Yes, research shows that OCD may run in families, as genes play a significant role in OCD emergence and development. But genes are not the only thing responsible for causing the disorder. Instead, OCD emerges due to a combination of genetic and environmental factors.

In 2020, a group of experienced psychiatrists conducted a study that involved several families. Their work also looked at twins and found that if your parent or sibling is suffering from OCD, the chances that you will also develop OCD will be greater than average.

But researchers are still studying this area and believe that family history may play a role in whether or not you or someone else gets OCD at some point in your life. The consensus for experts is that if you developed OCD as a child, then there is a greater likelihood that genetics are involved compared to if you developed it as an adult.

Question #8: What really causes OCD?

Science cannot point to a clearly defined cause. But as it's now known that OCD can run in families, researchers in psychiatry and other related fields are constantly looking at variations in the genes of OCD patients. They hope these variations will help them clearly explain why someone gets OCD, and another person does not. But what exists are possible causes. It's not clear what causes OCD. A number of different factors may play a part, including: family history, differences in the brain, life events, and personality.

Nevertheless, genes don't tell the complete story. For example, identical twins with the same genetic material can be different. As a result, one might have OCD while the other will not.

When it comes to the environment, it isn't really clear what causes OCD. In some cases, particularly among children, it could be because of a reaction to an infection. But this is still uncertain in most instances. As a teenager, painful experiences in your life can lead to symptoms appearing or even becoming worse. However, it still isn't clear if they actually cause OCD to someone vulnerable to it. Or they probably just become worse or amplify an already existing condition.

What's more, constant changes in a person's hormones also influence OCD. Adolescence is the most common period of onset. However, females have reported that their symptoms worsened with their menstrual cycle or even during pregnancy.

So, in summary, no clearly defined factors are essentially responsible for OCD. But, yes, it runs in families, and stressful environments can trigger it to start in one in every three people.

But then, scientists also believe that a neurotransmitter called serotonin may play a role in teens having OCD. Neurotransmitters are chemical messengers in your body, and their job is to take messages from a nerve cell in your body to the next across a space. These messages help you move your limbs, keep your heart beating, feel sensations, and receive and respond to the information your body gets from other parts and the environment.

Some scientific studies show that parents who overprotect their kids unknowingly increase their children's risk of developing OCD. However, considering everything holistically, your upbringing may not necessarily be a factor of your OCD.

Question #9: Does OCD mean being a neat freak?

Teens who are "neat freaks" may not have OCD. Sometimes, they are neat freaks by choice and not because their compulsions and obsessions influenced their behavior. However, it could be OCD if the teen becomes excessively concerned about contamination or neatness.

But if you are a teen who likes keeping things clean, we can accept that it is your personality and not OCD. People often see OCD patients as anyone who is neat, keeps their rooms in order, and maintains very strict hygiene. So it has become a common part of our active vocabulary. It is common to hear many teens say, "My OCD is so, so, and so…" Whereas it might just be their choices or personality. If you look at it from a medical viewpoint, you'll see that they are just misusing the term.

Question #10: Do obsessions lead to violent behavior?

Some obsessions have violent behaviors that aren't within the control of the teen dealing with OCD. All obsessions experienced by teens with OCD are involuntary and unwanted—these teens aren't intentionally violent or aggressive. Instead, their aggressive obsessions disturb them, making them act in ways that contradict their true personality. In psychology, this is called "ego-dystonic."

The compulsions teens with OCD perform to address the obsession do NOT include acting out the obsessive thoughts. Instead, their compulsions make them afraid of acting out those thoughts. That is why they do the opposite to neutralize or end the obsession instead of being violent. For example, teens with OCD will instead check to see that no one is hurt. Or they will walk very carefully to ensure they don't hit someone mistakenly.

Most of us are guilty of using the word "obsessed" to describe someone whose mind is preoccupied with just a person or an idea. In some instances, we associate it with stalking. But this type of obsession isn't the same as the types found in people with OCD.

Question #11: Is OCD treatable?

OCD doesn't have a cure yet, but you can be treated using different effective treatment methods, like cognitive behavioral therapy (CBT) and medication. A common starting point for most teens with OCD is to do CBT while taking medication.

According to research, this combined therapy approach is probably the most effective strategy to reduce OCD symptoms.

Also, if they combine psychotherapy and medication correctly, OCD symptoms can improve substantially for most teens, usually by 60–70%. But in some cases, only one of them is used.

Nevertheless, researchers are doing their best to find ways to help those who aren't improving sufficiently using existing treatments

Some people with OCD also have other mental disorders. For example, there are cases where OCD patients suffer from clinical anxiety, depression, and body dysmorphic disorder. In this disorder (dysmorphic disorder), the patient thinks that some parts of their body aren't normal. So specialists often consider other conditions before deciding on which treatment is suitable, and different types of treatment for these other disorders will be combined with treatment for OCD in this situation.

Question #12: How effective are treatments for OCD?

As I said earlier, CBT is also an effective OCD treatment method. Patients with OCD who are responsive to only medication usually show a 40 to 60% reduction in their OCD symptoms. Meanwhile, those who are responsive to CBT usually report that they have experienced between 60 to 80% reduction in their OCD symptoms.

So, in summary, there is always professional help through behavioral therapy and medication for people with OCD, including teenagers. And data shows that at least 3 out of 4 people who try CBT gradually improve. However, one in four OCD patients may experience relapse eventually. Although symptoms will reduce for 6 out of 10 people who use medications (often antidepressants), around 50% of them will experience relapse once they stop taking medication.

Some people try self-help to treat themselves; it is an essential aspect of the recovery journey. This book, for instance, provides you with some structured exercises you can try. But along with that, there are structured DVDs or self-help books that can help too. Nevertheless, it is always helpful to speak to someone you trust. For example, if your obsessive thoughts are related to religion or faith, talking to a religious leader may make sense for you.

Question #13: What's the difference between OCD and OCPD?

Although they sound and look alike, OCD and OCPD are not the same conditions. However, you or someone else can have both. According to the Journal of Personality Assessment, between 2 and 7% of the population have OCPD. OCD is a mental health condition where you struggle with obsessions and compulsions, and it sometimes looks like obsessive-compulsive personality disorder (OCPD). Still, teens with the personality disorder OCPD do not involve themselves in rituals. This disorder impacts their personality and more areas in their lives.

Teens with OCPD tend to have an extreme desire for control, perfection, and order, which can significantly affect their relationships with family and friends. Usually, they aren't aware of this, even when it is obvious to others.

Question #14: What can make OCD worse?

As I stated earlier, OCD may involve symptoms of anxiety. And if your stress increases, your OCD may worsen. According to a particular study, you might find that even the so-called good "stress"—like the feeling you get before starting a new school or after seeing a brilliant science result—can worsen your symptoms.

Other factors, like fatigue and lack of sleep, contribute too. What's more, if you stop your OCD medications suddenly, your symptoms might worsen. So always consult with your doctor before stopping or changing your medication.

CONCLUSION

> "Healing takes time, and asking for help is a courageous step."
>
> — MARISKA HARGITAY

Obsessive-compulsive disorder affects people of all ages and walks of life, and people who experience OCD are usually stuck in a web of obsessions and compulsions. But these obsessive thoughts and compulsive behaviors aren't limited to people with obsessive-compulsive disorder. Most people experience obsessive thoughts or compulsions, and sometimes even both. But that doesn't necessarily mean they have OCD.

For someone to be diagnosed with OCD, there must be an extreme cycle of compulsions and obsessions that eats a lot of their time (usually more than an hour each day), causes them extreme distress, or affects important activities and values.

Many factors are responsible for why OCD is becoming more common among teens. As a teenager, you are at the stage of your life where the world begins to open up to you like a strange new book. Things you never saw before start to appear, and the ones you have known before begin to mean something different to you. This is due to changes in your brain, but your brain isn't the only physiological aspect of change you will experience—your body, too, will change.

These changes cause issues like uncertainty, identity crisis, and a new sense of self, which OCD may build on. What's more, these issues are simply materials for your mind to obsess about. Unlike experienced adults who have learned to make educated guesses about these issues, you are still at the learning stage as a teen. So, you may often feel paralyzed with anxiety because you are unsure if your best guess will turn out right.

Nobody gets excited about discovering they have a mental disorder, especially because of stigma. As a result, many teens living with OCD go on with their lives without getting a diagnosis. They have to endure in silence while everyone else mocks them for their "weird" behavior, which makes it harder for them to be open about their situations. But this shouldn't be the case. It is always advisable to talk to someone you can trust. So find a therapist, family member, teacher, or spiritual/religious leader to share your feelings with, depending on their experience to help you understand your feelings.

As I've said several times, OCD isn't only about being a "neat freak," obsessing about contamination, or arranging things. For example, some teens with OCD experience violent, sexual, or moral obsessions. And they try to avoid these obsessions by doing mental rituals such as mental reviews, self-assurance, and thought neutralizations.

You may find yourself consistently in your head a lot, and people around you might misinterpret this as depression or attention deficit disorder. Some people may conclude that you are simply just being stubborn. That is why your family must be fully aware and completely involved in your treatment.

But fixating on your thoughts and performing certain rituals aren't the only signs that you might have OCD. Some teens start experiencing academic difficulties because of their OCD. For example, it affects their ability to read, count, or even focus during classes. And this further emphasizes the need for us to spread awareness so that teens are not misjudged as academically poor when they are not. Your teachers can design a better teaching strategy for you to learn more effectively.

The best approach to creating awareness is to share information about OCD and ensure that resources are readily available and accessible. Governments and experts like us are doing our bit through books like this and sensitizing teens living with OCD in your community. Also, to help teens with OCD around you, show them unconditional love. Do not judge or be mean to them. Instead, let them know how and where they can receive treatment and share your knowledge with them. You can also visit nearby OCD foundations for more help, counseling, and treatment information.

The truth is that, even under the best circumstances, being a teenager isn't easy. Your teenage life is where the world really opens to you, and you start getting several shocks. For instance, you understand bullying better, peer and societal pressures increase significantly, and school becomes more demanding. So it's normal for your anxiety levels to rise. But this is where the DBT comes in.

DBT can help you in several different ways, but first is that it can help you develop the skill of acceptance. Many teens dealing with OCD struggle to accept their experiences, leaving them with endless mental and emotional distress as they try to neutralize or suppress negative thoughts and emotions. DBT also teaches you how to avoid judging your feelings and help you deal with the things that cause you stress. In the long run, this will improve your happiness and quality of life.

In the end, it is very possible to deal with your OCD and eventually recover from it. But to do this, you must believe in yourself and approach your treatment with all the positivity you can muster. Remember that you are already a hero. You don't have to drop from Krypton, be raised in Smallville, and wear a cape to be a hero. Once you are brave enough to face your physical battles, you are already a hero.

Heroes go through various challenges and can become overwhelmed at some point. Still, their will, determination, and resilience always give them an edge over the villain. So, as you fight your OCD, imagine you are your favorite comic hero, and your OCD is your archnemesis in that story. But guess what? The hero always wins, right? And so will you.

Remember Wendy's story in Chapter 5? She faced her OCD despite the difficult circumstances she found herself in. And if Wendy could do it, so will you. Yes, you can.

So, take this chance to overcome your OCD and become the best version of yourself. And please don't forget to share this book with your friends and leave a review.

To your success,

Cross Border Books.

REFERENCES

Achieve Medical (2022). Paced Breathing. https://bit.ly/3GA716N

American Academy of Child and Adolescent Psychiatry (2018). Obsessive-Compulsive Disorder in Children and Adolescents. http://bit.ly/3hSiZ18

APA (2022). What Is Obsessive-Compulsive Disorder? https://psychiatry.org/patients-families/obsessive-compulsive-disorder/what-is-obsessive-compulsive-disorder

A-Z health (2022). Obsessive compulsive disorder (OCD) in children and teenagers. OCD in children & teenagers | Raising Children Network

Beauty and the Borderline (2022). Distress Tolerance Pros and Cons. Distress Tolerance: Pros & Cons | Beauty and the Borderline (wordpress.com)

Behavioral Research and Therapy Clinics (2022). Dialectical Behavior Therapy. University of Washington. https://depts.washington.edu/uwbrtc/about-us/dialectical-behavior-therapy/

Boyce, B. (2011). The Healing Power of Mindfulness. Mindful. https://www.mindful.org/the-healing-power-of-mindfulness/

Bray, S. (2013). Emotion Regulation in Dialectical Behavior Therapy http://bit.ly/3Gtq3vg

Compitus, K. (2020). What Are Distress Tolerance Skills? The Ultimate DBT Toolkit https://positivepsychology.com/distress-tolerance-skills/

Cleveland Clinic (2022). Dialectical Behavior Therapy (DBT) https://my.clevelandclinic.org/health/treatments/22838-dialectical-behavior-therapy-dbt

COGNITIVE BEHAVIORAL THERAPY LOS ANGELES (2022). Mindfulness from a DBT Perspective https://cogbtherapy.com/cbt-blog/mindfulness-in-dbt

DBT Skills Group (2022). The Four Skill Modules. https://dbtskillsgroupnj.com/four-skill-modules/

Elias, M.J. (2018). Pros and Cons of Mindfulness in SEL https://www.edutopia.org/article/pros-and-cons-mindfulness-sel

Kerry, C. (2022). Benefits of Mindfulness. Verywell Mind. https://www.verywellmind.com/the-benefits-of-mindfulness-5205137

Kluger, J. (2022). Pandemic Anxiety Is Fueling OCD Symptoms—Even for

People Without the Disorder https://time.com/6140256/ocd-covid-19-anxiety/

Made of Millions (2022). Mindfulness and OCD https://www.madeofmillions.com/ocd/mindfulness

Manhattan Psychology Group (2022). DIALECTICAL BEHAVIOR THERAPY (DBT) DISTRESS TOLERANCE SKILLS: TIPP SKILLS. https://manhattanpsychologygroup.com/dbt-tipp-skills/

Medical News Today (2022). Everything to know about dialectical behavioral therapy https://www.medicalnewstoday.com/articles/everything-to-know-about-dialectical-behavioral-therapy

MHS (2022). Dialectical Behavior Therapy for OCD, does it Work? https://www.mhs-dbt.com/blog/help-ocd-with-dbt/

NIH (2022). Transforming the understanding and treatment of mental illnesses. https://www.nimh.nih.gov/health/topics/obsessive-compulsive-disorder-ocd

NHS (2022). Overview - obsessive compulsive disorder (OCD) https://www.nhs.uk/mental-health/conditions/obsessive-compulsive-disorder-ocd/overview/

Pierce, L. (2021). Dialectical Behavior Therapy for OCD: Another Alternative When Exposure Therapy Doesn't Work. Verywell Mind. https://www.verywellmind.com/ocd-dbt-skills-2510652

Sheppard Pratt (2022). 5 Things to Understand about Teens and OCD. https://www.sheppardpratt.org/news-views/story/5-things-to-understand-about-teens-and-ocd/

Taproot Therapy. (2020). Dialectical Behavior Therapy Skills. https://www.taproottherapynyc.com/blog-dialectical-behavior-therapy-skills/dbt-skills-the-6-core-mindfulness-skills

Therapist Aid (2022). DBT Distress Tolerance Skills https://www.therapistaid.com/therapy-worksheet/dbt-distress-tolerance-skills

Vaughn, S. (2021). History of DBT: Origins and Foundations https://psychotherapyacademy.org/dbt/history-of-dialectical-behavioral-therapy-a-very-brief-introduction/

Sunrise (2022). DBT Distress Tolerance Skills: Your 6-Skill Guide to Navigate Emotional Crises. https://sunrisertc.com/distress-tolerance-skills/

Juby, B. (2022). Why emotional self-regulation is important and how to do it. https://www.medicalnewstoday.com/articles/emotional-self-regulation#seeking-help

Chowdhury, M.R. (2019). Emotional Regulation: 6 Key Skills to Regulate Emotions. https://positivepsychology.com/emotion-regulation/

ieso (2020). What are intrusive thoughts? https://www.iesohealth.com/wellbeing-blog/what-are-intrusive-thoughts

Butterfield, A. (2019). INTRUSIVE THOUGHTS. https://theocdandanxietycenter.com/intrusive-thoughts/

Nystrom Associates (2022). Interpersonal Effectiveness https://www.nystromcounseling.com/specialty-areas/interpersonal-effectiveness/

Course Hero, 2022.Pros and cons of using interpersonal effectiveness https://www.coursehero.com/file/p461i65/Pros-and-Cons-of-Using-Interpersonal-Effectiveness-Skills-Due-Date-Name-Week/

Schenk, L. (2022). Identify 6 Key Interpersonal Skills. Mindfulness Muse. https://www.mindfulnessmuse.com/interpersonal-relationships/identify-6-key-interpersonal-skills

Anxiety Canada (2022). Obsessive-Compulsive Disorder www.anxiety-canada.com

OCD UK (2022). What are compulsions? https://www.ocduk.org/ocd/compulsions/

Healthline (2022). Understanding the Difference Between Obsessions and Compulsions https://www.healthline.com/health/obsession-vs-compulsion#examples

OCD Research Clinic (2022). Frequently asked questions about OCD https://medicine.yale.edu/psychiatry/ocd/aboutocd/faqs/

Brain and Behavior (2022). Obsessive-Compulsive Disorder (OCD) FAQs https://www.bbrfoundation.org/faq/frequently-asked-questions-about-ocd